84.33 Men
enhard, Francha Roffe.
nternet issues

$ 20.95

Internet Issues

Pirates, Censors, and Cybersquatters

Francha Roffé Menhard

Enslow Publishers, Inc.

40 Industrial Road	PO Box 38
Box 398	Aldershot
Berkeley Heights, NJ 07922	Hants GU12 6BP
USA	UK

http://www.enslow.com

*This book is dedicated to my mother, who knew I
would be a writer even before I was born.*

Library of Congress Cataloging-in-Publication Data

Roffé Menhard, Francha.
    Internet issues : pirates, censors, and cybersquatters / Francha
Roffé Menhard.
        p. cm. — (Issues in focus)
    Includes bibliographic references and index.
    ISBN 0-7660-1687-0
    1. Internet—Juvenile literature. [1. Internet.] I. Title. II. Issues
in focus (Hillside, N.J.)
    TK5105.875.I57 R64   2000
    384.3'3--dc21

                                        00-012461

10 9 8 7 6 5 4 3 2

To Our Readers: We have done our best to make sure all Internet
addresses in this book were active and appropriate when we went to
press. However, the author and the publisher have no control over and
assume no liability for the material available on those Internet sites or
on other Web sites they may link to. Any comments or suggestions can
be sent by e-mail to comments@enslow.com or to the address on the
back cover.

Contents

1

A Little Bit of History

In the 1980s, physicist Tim Berners-Lee had an idea: "Suppose all the information stored on computers everywhere were linked. Suppose I could program my computer to create a space in which anything could be linked to anything."[1] What if he could find a way to connect computers around the world, no matter what operating system they used?

His idea grew out of a common problem. He could not remember where information was stored at the CERN Particle Physics Laboratory in Switzerland where he worked. So Berners-Lee turned his idea into a computer program he called Enquire. Enquire assigned an address to each "page" of information on CERN's computers. Berners-Lee could type in a word or two, and voila! His program would lead him to relevant information.

With that simple beginning, the World Wide Web was born.

The Internet had been around since the 1960s, when the government felt the need for an alternative communications system that could survive a nuclear war. The new system, then called ARPANet, was decentralized, connecting computers with regular telephone lines. ARPANet would route around any damage and keep the lines of communication open.

At the start, scientists, professors, and the military used ARPANet. Then it caught on with other university professors and students. They found ARPANet a cheap and easy way to share information.

In the 1980s, people began to realize that they could connect their computers together using telephone lines. Small, local computer bulletin boards—places in cyberspace where computer users could leave messages for each other—sprang up; then huge, commercial ones. Prodigy, the first commercial computer bulletin board, opened its virtual doors in 1988. Other commercial computer bulletin boards, Compuserve, Genie, and America Online, followed. These services let ordinary people gossip, share recipes, and discuss politics, to create an online community.

America was ready for more. America was ready for the Internet. But the Internet was still a bare bones affair. There was no way for average people to find the information they wanted. That is where Tim Berners-Lee and the World Wide Web came in. By then, Berners-Lee was working at the Massachusetts Institute of Technology. In May 1990, he had turned his idea of ten years before into the computer software that would run the World Wide Web.[2]

The Internet and the World Wide Web

The Internet is a worldwide network of computer networks. It is a jumble of cables, computers, routers, and other hardware. At any given time, the Internet connects some 15 million users on seven continents. The Internet carries data and makes the exchange of information possible.

Still, not many people used the Internet before the World Wide Web. Internet users had to type in a long, complicated series of numbers to get the information they wanted. And it was difficult to find anything unless they already knew where it was.

The World Wide Web changed all that. Prodigy and America Online subscribers found the Web comfortable and easy to use. Soon people began to skip the big bulletin boards completely and accessed the Internet directly. Now what people saw when they logged on was something like a television screen, only better. With a click of the mouse, the Web's hyperlinks—highlighted words or pictures—magically transported Internet users to related information— news stories, e-mail, and audio or video files. And the World Wide Web was interoperable. It could link

Once upon a not-so-long-ago, instant communication was an idea believed in only by science fiction fans. Now, people who belong to an Internet service can communicate instantly worldwide via a keyboard.

anyone, no matter what kind of computer or software was used.

Today, many people think the Internet and the World Wide Web are the same thing. They are not. The Web is just one way of exchanging information on the Internet. E-mail and IRC (Internet Relay Chat) are others. The Internet can exist without the World Wide Web, but the Web could not exist without the Internet.[3]

Still, the Web has become the public face of the Internet. And whatever the technical difference, for most people, the Web is the Internet. This book uses the terms interchangeably when referring to using the World Wide Web to access the Internet.

Future of the Internet and the World Wide Web

Tim Berners-Lee created the World Wide Web to connect people around the world, to help people work together more easily. But his creation has grown too big for him to control. What will the Internet become in the future? "The Web is what we make it," says Berners-Lee.

"'We' being the people who read, the people who teach children how to surf the web, the people who put information up on the web. Particularly the people who put up links."[4]

In the next ten years, governments, businesses, and individuals will weigh in on the issues that face the Internet: equality, control, privacy, and trust.[5]

At present, there is no equality on the Internet. The rich can easily access the Internet. The poor cannot. Businesses and governments are already working toward more equality. They are working to bridge the digital divide—that gulf between computer and Internet access for the rich and the poor. But most people in the world still do not have computer access, let alone access to the Internet.

At the same time, governments, businesses, and individuals are scrambling to control the Net. Each group has a strong opinion on Internet censorship and taxation and copyright. Ordinary people are demanding more protection of their privacy, even as business thrives on knowing everything about every Web visitor.

And everyone wants to make the Internet a safe place. Parents, schools, and libraries debate the best ways to make the Internet safe for children. Police work to protect the citizens of the Internet—netizens—from scam artists and online criminals. At the same time, many people worry that making the Internet safe will also make it less free.

The debate over Internet issues will continue. Courts will make some of the decisions. Lawmakers will decide others. The new Internet industry will decide still others. But ordinary netizens will also have a say in shaping the future of the Internet.

2

The Digital Divide: Falling Through the (Inter)Net

Sometime during 1999, thirteen-year-old Myra Jodie finished her classwork early at her middle school on the Navajo reservation in Shiprock, Arizona. Her teacher let her sign on to the Net on the classroom computer. Myra found her way to AWZ.com, a teen site. AWZ.com was having a contest, and Myra entered it.

Busy with school, sports, and chores, Myra forgot all about the contest until February 2000. An AWZ.com employee could not reach her by e-mail. School was out, and no one checked her teacher's e-mail. So he called her school and made

11

arrangements to meet her and give her the prize she had won: a blueberry and white iMac laptop computer complete with modem. Great, right? Yes, except that Myra's family had no phone. In fact, the nearest public phone is ten miles away at the grocery store.[1]

When President Bill Clinton visited Shiprock, a far-flung community of about eight thousand, he was the first president still in office ever to visit a Navajo reservation. The Navajo Nation has a population of two hundred thousand spread out on twenty-eight thousand square miles.[2] On the reservation, only 22.5 percent of homes have phones. Only 37 percent have electricity.[3]

East Palo Alto

East Palo Alto, California, population twenty-five thousand, is the Cinderella of Silicon Valley—the heart of the computer industry. Sixty-five percent of the schoolchildren speak limited English. Eighty percent are poor enough to qualify for free lunch at school. Eighty-five percent are minorities.[4] Schools average one computer for every twenty-eight students—about one computer per classroom.[5]

Nearby Palo Alto is East Palo Alto's wealthy stepsister. In 1999, Palo Alto schools boasted one computer for every five students.[6] Palo Alto students are more likely to have Internet access at home, too. The city of Palo Alto is working to provide high-speed fiber optic Internet connections to every home, along with electricity.[7]

The Gap

At the birth of the Internet age, many analysts assumed that the computer would be a leveling agent, granting anyone with a modem equal access to information. But studies have shown troubling technology gaps developing along racial and class lines.[8]

Households with incomes above $75,000 are twenty times more likely to have access to the Internet than those at the lowest income levels. Americans living in rural areas are less likely to have access, regardless of income. And whites are more likely to have access from home than African Americans or Hispanics.

In 1989, low-income households in central cities had the lowest telephone subscription rates (72.6 percent, compared to 73.8 percent in rural areas and 76.2 percent in urban areas). In 1998, those least likely to have telephone service were low-income families living in rural areas (76.3 percent, compared to 78.7 percent in central cities and 79.2 percent in urban areas). What kind of people own telephones? People with higher incomes, whites, people over fifty-five. Who does not? African Americans and Hispanics, single-parent households, and people under age twenty-five.

What kind of people own personal computers? People with jobs, high incomes, and college degrees; married couples with children, and households in the western United States. Households with lower incomes and education levels, Southerners and people who live in rural areas, and people under the age of twenty-five are less likely to own one. Rural African-American households are the least likely to have a home computer.[10]

The Government Takes Action

The 1996 Telecommunications Act authorized $2.25 billion annually to help schools, libraries, and rural health care facilities pay for Internet connections. It also provided affordable telephone service in rural areas.

President Clinton crafted a Year 2000 plan to help bridge the digital divide. The plan authorized $300 million for training teachers, creating community technology centers in low-income areas, and helping low-income families get computers and Internet access. The government planned $2 billion more in tax cuts for businesses that they hoped would help bridge the digital divide.[11]

And Americans would also fund new telephone service to about three hundred thousand homes on Indian reservations with a .04 percent tax on long distance calls. Basic telephone service would cost Indian families about a dollar a month.[12] Some people complained loudly when the tax first appeared on their telephone bills. One letter to the editor represented the opinion of many. Its writer complained about the National Access Contribution and asked why current telephone users should pay to provide rural areas with telephone and Internet service.[13]

But requiring taxpayers to help pay for universal

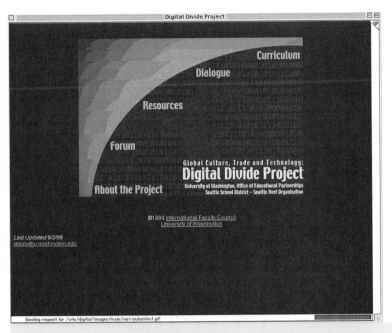

In 1999, the University of Washington and the Seattle School District launched the Digital Divide Project to familiarize students with the complexities of the digital divide.

service is nothing new. Established in the 1930s, the Federal Communications Commission pushed the telephone company—back then there was only one, AT&T—to provide affordable service to all customers.

After the breakup of AT&T, the FCC helped private telephone companies keep their charges in line with those of AT&T customers. In 1985, the FCC began a program to provide phone service for low-income consumers. Until 1996, long distance companies paid for that. The FCC increased the number of companies that contributed to universal service, and in 1998, began to require all telecommunications carriers to contribute.

Digital Divide: Really?

Some people also complained about President Clinton's universal Internet Access program. They argued that there was no need for the government to get involved. Forrester Research reported that the gap between black and white computer owners is narrowing on its own. PCs used to cost thousands of dollars. Today, powerful computers can cost less than one thousand dollars. Used computers can cost just hundreds. Not counting the cost of a computer, Internet access costs less than basic cable television in most places. People can choose Internet access over cable television, but most do not.

The digital divide narrowed significantly in the four years after 1996, when the Clinton Administration first began to publicize it. By the year 2000, according to a Forrester Research study, more Asian (74 percent) and Hispanic households (55 percent) used the Internet, compared to 45 percent of white and 35 percent of African-American households.[14] The racial divide, it seemed, had narrowed. The economic divide—the gap between rich and poor—remained wide.

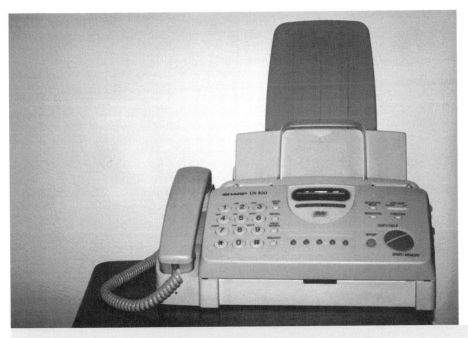

Many Americans consider cable television a necessity. Not so many consider computers, e-mail units, and fax machines necessities.

Private Industry Takes Action

Private industry has had great success in building bridges across the digital divide. Lake Valley Middle School in rural northwestern New Mexico used to connect to the Internet via telephone and modem. The connection was slow. Students sometimes waited up to forty minutes for Web sites to load.

Then Tachyon, Inc., a wireless Internet service company, set up a thirty-thousand dollar satellite system at the school. Now, Web pages load in seconds. The Office of Indian Education would like

Private industry has come to the assistance of poor schools in some parts of the United States, doing such things as setting up satellite systems to allow broader access.

to hook up all of its 185 schools to the Internet via satellite.

Meanwhile, the software company Microsoft donated more than $2.7 million in cash and software to enhance computer instruction at eight tribal colleges across the West. In Detroit, two lawyers put their careers on hold in order to start a program that draws inner-city youths to computer-training sessions with after-school sports. The governor of Maine worked to create an endowment that would buy laptops for all seventh graders. And the people behind netnoir.com, a site marketing products to the African-American community, have begun training low-income San Francisco youths for high-tech careers.[15]

But it is not enough for companies and organizations to reach out to students. Students have a responsibility, too. If the United States is to stay on the right side of the world technological divide, students today must choose to study hard and learn the skills that tomorrow will require.

The Worldwide Digital Divide

Even as Americans worked to bridge the digital divide at home, much of the rest of the world was being left behind. The United States and Canada have about 5 percent of the world's population, but almost half of all Internet users live there.[16] Only 12 percent of Internet users live outside Western Europe, Australia, Japan, and other industrialized countries.[17]

Central and Eastern European countries lag behind Western Europe in telephone service and Internet access. For example, in Romania, Poland, and Russia, fewer than 18 percent of homes had telephones in 1996. Bulgaria, Croatia, and the Czech Republic averaged about 30 percent. Bosnia-Herzegovina had under 10 percent.[18]

One major barrier to telephone and Internet usage in many countries is old phone lines and old technology. Would-be telephone owners find themselves on waiting lists. Those who do have a phone say that their service is poor. Many still use party lines. They have to share their phone lines with neighbors. If one neighbor is using the phone, no one else can call out or

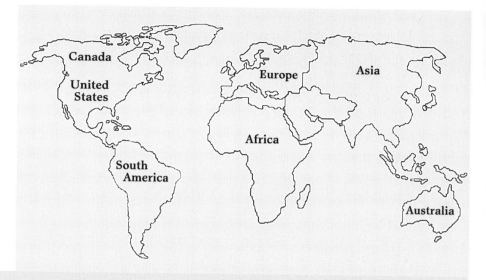

The United States and Canada make up only 5 percent of the
world's population but account for half of its computer access.

receive calls. But anyone on the party line can listen
in. There is little privacy. There are no superfast
all-the-time connections that some users in the United
States have. Everyone must depend on a telephone and
modem to access the Internet.

Another barrier to usage is the way governments
allow phone companies to do business. Telephone
customers in most countries pay by the minute for
phone calls. That limits recreational Web surfing. But
citizens of Central and Eastern European countries
are letting their governments know that they want to
be able to access the Internet easily. And Internet use
in those countries is growing rapidly.

Internet access is also growing rapidly in Latin
America—more than 40 percent a year.[19] Still,

universal access will not be easy to achieve. In 1998, only about 12 percent of Latin Americans had telephones, according to the United Nations' Development Report 2000.

In much of the rest of the world, however, the situation is much less encouraging. For people who lack shelter, food, clean water, and health care, Internet access is low on their list of priorities. Fewer than 2 percent of the world's people are connected to the Internet. In fact, worldwide, fewer than 20 percent have ever even heard a dial tone.[20]

In East Asia, with its population of over a billion, fewer than one percent of people have telephones.[21] In South Asia, which includes India, fewer than 2 percent had telephones in 1998,[22] and fewer than one percent of people are online.[23] The numbers are even lower in Southeast Asia.

The continent of Africa, with its 739 million people, had only fourteen thousand telephone lines in 1999 and only about a million Internet users. There are more telephone lines in Tokyo than on the continent of Africa, and more than ten times as many Internet users on America Online.[24]

Still, the world digital divide is narrowing bit by bit. Governments and businesses around the world are working to provide access to the Internet. From the crowded streets of Istanbul, Turkey, to the jungles of the Amazon in South America, people are heading for cybercafés where they can sit and drink coffee and connect to the Internet for an hourly fee.

3

Censoring
the Internet

Vu was born during the middle of the
Vietnam War, but the war did not intrude
on his home in Saigon. His sister worked
at the U.S. Embassy, and Vu learned to
love to read.

In 1975, the United States withdrew
from Vietnam. The Communists took over.
Things got bad. Vu's family was black-
listed because of his sister's former job.
Neighbors spied on his family. There was
never enough food. Still, Vu could always
lose himself in a book.

Then the police came and burned his
books. Vu knew there was no life for him

in Vietnam, and he tried to escape. In 1981, he made it. He found a new home in the United States, but he missed his family and his homeland. One day, Vu saw a television documentary on Vietnam. He saw how poor the farmers were and how hard they worked with their bare hands. He could not stop crying.

Vu promised himself that he would one day return to Vietnam to do something good for the people of his homeland. He thought providing Internet access would be a valuable contribution. In 1996, Vu returned to Saigon. There, he and a partner set up the Tam Tam II, an Internet café. He and his partner had dreams of setting up a network of cybercafés that would link Vietnam to the rest of the world via the Internet.

By February 1997, between forty and sixty people came to the café every day. That is when Vietnam's Interior Ministry intelligence officials shut him down. Why? Vu figured they may have thought his American partner was a CIA agent. Or perhaps government officials viewed him as an overseas Vietnamese "radical," using the Internet to cause trouble. Whatever the reason, police sealed Vu's computers in plastic. Half a year later, the café was still shuttered. The sign on the door of the café, faded with age, still read, "Café will be closed for a few days." No more free flow of information. Vu lost. The police state won. Censorship won.[1]

Fear of Surfing

The aging leaders of Vietnam see the Internet as a threat, and rightly so. Before the Internet, governments could control access to information. Today, e-mail and the Internet bring uncensored information into most countries, whether their governments like it or not. Most countries realize that if they want to compete economically with the rest of the world, they must open up access to the Internet.

Governments that fear the Internet try to control it in a number of ways. Some do not allow citizens access to cyberspace at all. China and Burma require Internet users to register their computers with the police. Vietnam licenses computers the way the United States licenses cars. Iraq and Saudi Arabia control Internet content with filters. The Sudanese and Syrians control content by owning the Internet service providers.

Many other countries control access to the Internet with high fees for use. In Cuba, for example, the average citizen has never keyed into the Internet or sent an e-mail. Columbus!, a Cuba Online of sorts, costs sixty dollars per month in U.S. dollars. The average monthly income in Cuba is equivalent to ten dollars in the United States.[2] Most people do not have access to U.S. dollars. And many governments have harsh laws that punish users and service providers for spreading false information, libeling national organizations, insulting national heroes, or encouraging what they consider social evils.

Things in Vietnam are changing slowly. The government no longer monitors all e-mail, and Vietnamese citizens can surf the Web at the Internet cafés that the government has not driven out of business.[3]

The Internet continues to open new opportunities to countries which have been traditionally poor. The Internet has improved education and science, and even tourism. Leaders around the world are learning that no matter how much they want to control their citizens, censorship is not the answer. Censorship of the Internet will only keep their countries poor and isolated.

Meanwhile, Back in the Land of the Free

People think that what makes the United States better than many other countries is the ability of its citizens to find information freely, without the government censoring what people read on the Internet. Right?

Not exactly. The United States also censors the Internet. Most government censorship is in libraries and schools in the name of protecting young people.

Asking the Hard Questions

Is it all right for libraries to censor the Internet? Does protecting children from pornographic, violent, and hate sites justify censorship? Holland, Michigan, was the first community to let its citizens vote on that issue. In February 2000, voters had to decide about a law that would require libraries to install special software to filter out unacceptable Internet content in order not to lose their funding.

Elaine Cioffi, sixty-two, voted for filtering information. "I just think that children really don't know what's for their own good," she said. "It may not be a really big problem at the library right now or in the future, but why take a chance?"[4] The community defeated the measure.

Students and anticensorship groups disagree for several reasons. First, they say, filters do not work. Filters often keep surfers from legitimate information. And the companies that make filtering software refuse to reveal just what it is they censor.

One anticensorship organization, Peacefire, argues that it is better for children to learn to deal with the dark side of the Internet than to lose their constitutional rights. That is why Peacefire developed programs to break the code of a number of other censorware programs, including CYBERsitter, Cyber Patrol, SurfWatch, Net Nanny, SmartFilter, WebSENSE, and BESS.[5]

Utah's Education Network (UEN), for example, uses SmartFilter to censor the Internet in the state's public schools and some libraries. UEN banned access to huge chunks of noncontroversial information. UEN filters for five categories: hate speech, drugs, sex, criminal skills, and gambling.

According to records obtained by the Censorware Project, the hate-speech filter triggered a ban on a scholarly paper about Nazi Germany. The drug filter denied access to the National Institute of Health's brochure, "Marijuana: Facts for Teens." The sex filter banned access to the Web site of the Mormon Church, ironic in Utah, home of the church.

The criminal-skills filter blocked the Declaration of Independence.[6] And the gambling filter blocked author Walter Wager's home page. Other

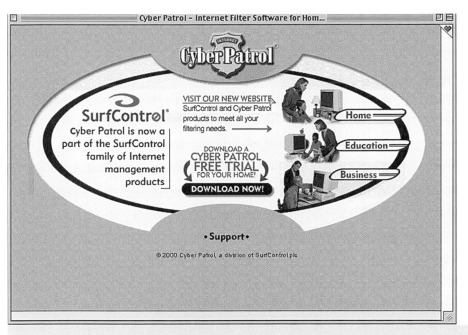

Cyber Patrol is just one of a number of software programs developed to help parents and others censor what their children can view on the Web.

blocked sites carried the U.S. Constitution, the Bible, the Book of Mormon, the Koran, *The Adventures of Sherlock Holmes*, George Washington's Farewell Address, The Mayflower Compact, Shakespeare's plays, and *Seventeen* magazine.[7]

Who was deciding which sites to ban? Irrational librarians? Paranoid teachers?

Neither. According to the Censorware Project, the computer made the decision. No human would consider the Iowa State police site or Walter Wager's home page dangerous. But a computer would. A computer might object to the Declaration of Independence as encouraging rebellion. A human would know better. A computer cannot tell the difference between wagering as gambling and Wager as a last name. A human can.

In fact, SmartFilter banned the entire Internet Wiretap server that hosts the Declaration of Independence, along with hundreds of literary, government, and religious Web pages. Why? Michael Sims of the Censorware Project assumes it is because of a quotation on its home page:

> Printer's ink has been running a race against gunpowder these many, many years. Ink is handicapped in a way, because you can blow up a man with gunpowder in half a second, while it may take twenty years to blow him up with a book. But the gunpowder destroys itself along with its victim, while a book can keep exploding for centuries.[8]

Whatever its purpose, censorship is wrong, said the Censorware Project: "When the Declaration of Independence is banned from the citizens of Saudi Arabia so that they won't get ideas, we call it culturally backward. And when it is banned from our own public libraries by our own government, then what do we call it?"[9]

This view of censorship was also held by newspaper reporter Richard Pothier, an active online debater who died in 1995. He wrote:

> Censorship is never the answer to unpopular opinions. The "court of public opinion" makes its own judgment. Intolerance, bigotry and

other forms of stupidity are seen for what they are.[10]

The Communications Decency Act

February 1996 saw a new nationwide push to censor the Internet. The Communications Decency Act (CDA) made it a crime to make "indecent" or "patently offensive" material available to minors on the Internet.[11] People who violated the law could spend two years in jail and pay huge fines.[12]

Netizens rushed to protest. Webmasters worldwide changed the background of their sites to black to mourn the death of freedom of speech. The American Civil Liberties Union (ACLU) and dozens of online companies, publishers, libraries, and others joined in a lawsuit against the CDA. The law would make speech on the Internet a crime, they said. The Bill of Rights protected that same speech in real life. Why not on the Internet?

And what was "indecent" anyway? Who would define it? What was "patently offensive"? Who would define what was "harmful to minors"? Would it be a crime to post a picture of Michelangelo's sculpture of the naked David on the Web? Would a paper about breast cancer or colon surgery be illegal?

The Court Rules

On June 12, 1996, a three-judge panel in Philadelphia issued a preliminary injunction blocking enforcement of the CDA. The Internet, the court ruled, was "the most participatory form of mass speech yet developed." It deserved "the highest protection from government intrusion."[13]

The Justice Department immediately appealed the ruling to the Supreme Court. Its June 1997 ruling struck down the CDA. Justice John Paul Stevens wrote the majority opinion: "The interest in encouraging freedom of expression in a democratic society outweighs any . . . benefit of censorship." The First Amendment protects speech on the Internet in the same way that it protects books and newspapers.

Perhaps the only way to make sure teens are not seeing anything they should not see on the Web is to stand and watch over their shoulders.

Justice Stevens also found serious problems with the law. The CDA was too vague. People could not be sure if it was legal to discuss birth control, homosexuality, or prison rape. The law was also too broad. With as many as 60 million people online, no one could be sure that their words would not reach a child somewhere. The CDA infringed on the speech rights of adults in the name of protecting children. This was not an acceptable reason to allow censorship.[14]

Censoring Student Writing

Seventeen-year-old Woodland High School student Brandon Beussink posted a Web site that consisted of criticisms of his school and his principal. He used his parents' computer after school hours to create the site.

His principal was not amused. School officials

ordered Brandon to take down the Web site, and he did. In February of 1998, his principal suspended Brandon for ten days. Because of the suspension, Brandon failed the semester and was not able to graduate with his class.

The Supreme Court has heard a number of cases dealing with the censorship of student writing.

Brandon and the Eastern Missouri American Civil Liberties Union (ACLU) took the case to court. In December 1998, U.S. District Court Judge Rodney Sippel ruled that the Woodland School District in Marble Hill, Missouri, had trampled Brandon's First Amendment right of free speech. He ruled that the school district could not consider the suspension in calculating Brandon's grades. Shortly after Judge Sippel ruled, the school district settled the suit. School officials apologized to Brandon, removed the suspension from his record, and awarded him thirty thousand dollars.[15] The Supreme Court ruling, *Tinker v. Des Moines*, 1969, stated:

> It can hardly be argued that either students or teachers shed their constitutional rights to freedom of speech or expression at the schoolhouse gate. . . . In our system, state-operated schools may not be enclaves of totalitarianism. School officials do not possess absolute authority over their students. Students in school as well as out of school are "persons" under our Constitution. They are possessed of fundamental rights, which the State must respect. . . . They may not be confined to the expression of those sentiments that are officially approved.

United States courts have generally upheld students' rights to publish whatever they want, whether in print or in cyberspace, as long as they do it outside school. And schools can punish students who disrupt the educational process. But schools cannot punish students for personal Web sites simply because they do not like the content of a student's speech.

Of course, students are still responsible for what they write. If they make threats, publish false information about someone, or use another person's work without permission, students can be prosecuted. And at least one court has ruled that schools can punish students whose Web sites disrupt the educational process.

In March 2000, the Pennsylvania Commonwealth Court ruled against Justin Swidler, a student at Nitschmann Middle School in Bethlehem, Pennsylvania. Justin's online criticisms of his principal and algebra teacher had disrupted the educational process by causing emotional damage and "affecting other students' perceptions" of the principal and the teacher. The court also ruled that Justin's comments were a "legitimate threat," even though local police had refused to file charges against him.[16]

Brandon Beussink can only wonder at the irony of prosecuting students for expressing unpopular opinions. "We study history and we study the Constitution," he said, "but the school doesn't seem to think it applies to them."[17]

Nathan L. Essex, a dean at the University of Memphis, agrees that it is important to safeguard individual students' constitutional rights. "We should treat students fairly," he said, "not because the courts mandate it, but because it is the right thing to do."[18]

4

Who Controls the Internet?

Aaron Doades knew he was in big trouble the minute he read the letter from Black Entertainment Television (BET). If he did not shut down his rapcity.com Web site, BET's lawyers would go to court to shut him down. Aaron, an eighth grader who had started the rap fan Web site on America Online when he was ten, did not think that was fair.

When he was twelve, Aaron had registered his site, www.rapcity.com, with Network Solutions, the registry of Web addresses at that time. A couple of months later he saw an ad for BET's program, Rap City. Aaron knew that even though he had registered for rapcity.com first, BET owned the trademark. He would need BET's permission to continue to use Rap City and rapcity.com.

Aaron immediately wrote to BET, asking if he could continue to use Rap City as his site name. BET said no. He wrote again and asked if he could keep the domain name, www.rapcity.com, if he dropped Rap City as the title of his site and instead used "Tha Hood." BET did not answer.

Aaron changed the name of his site. Soon Tha Hood was making a name for itself. A search engine, Ask Jeeves, advertised on his site. A couple of independent record companies paid him a commission to sell their CDs on Tha Hood. In the summer of 1999, Aaron was earning about eight hundred dollars a month from his Web site.

That is when he got the letter from BET. Network Solutions shut Tha Hood down until Aaron and BET could resolve their dispute. Even after BET found out that Aaron was a teen, they did not back down. By registering BET's trademark, Rap City, as his domain name, Aaron had become a cybersquatter, the network said.

If Aaron wanted to, he could negotiate with BET for a license to use the trademark, a BET lawyer told him. At twelve, the boy was too young to sign a binding contract with the network, but the BET lawyer did not address that issue. Aaron decided he deserved compensation for losing his Web site. He offered to sell BET his Web address for one hundred thousand dollars. But BET said no. They offered him four thousand dollars. Aaron refused.

That is when Aaron's father filed a $10 million lawsuit against BET on his son's behalf. Of course, neither Mr. Doades nor Aaron expected to be awarded $10 million. They just used that big number to get people to pay attention to an important principle: Big companies should not push little ones around. BET and Network Solutions were working to get a judge to dismiss the suit.

Meanwhile, Aaron has not let BET stop him. He found a new address for Tha Hood. By the summer of 2000, Aaron's site was back up and running. The case against BET has been settled in Aaron's favor.[1]

Who Decides?

No one owns the Internet, it is true. But the Net is highly organized and even regulated. The Internet Engineering Task Force, or IETF, develops technical standards. The Internet Corporation for Assigned Names and Numbers, ICANN, keeps track of Internet names and numbers and oversees Web suffixes such as .com and .org. And the World Wide Web Consortium, W3C, works to keep the Web's languages and protocols compatible with one another. The consortium also works to keep the Web simple and expandable, and to keep it decentralized.

In general, these governing bodies date back to the early days of the Internet. They created themselves and, generally, they govern themselves. Anyone can join, and anyone can contribute. They make decisions by consensus, but more highly respected members may have a bigger say.

Domain Names and Cybersquatting

For years, scientists controlled domain names. But when the World Wide Web's popularity soared in the early 1990s, the U.S. government gave Network Solutions the job of registering domain names. In 1995, the U.S. government stopped paying for domain name registration, and Network Solutions started charging a $35 annual fee for registering domain names.

Domain names have become more valuable than anyone ever expected. Many online companies have made their domains the cornerstone of their business. Many companies use their corporate name or trademark in their domain name. For example, the grocery store Safeway has www.safeway.com as its homepage. A predictable Web address helps possible customers find a company's Web site easily.

But what happens when customers type in a company's name and get a blank page or a software company they have never heard of? They may take their business elsewhere. Realizing this, cybersquatters scooped up the names of big, successful companies— and offered them to the companies for large sums of money.[2] Cybersquatting means buying domain names that feature company names or popular trademarks, hoping that someone will pay a lot of money for them one day.

Some companies did pay cybersquatters a lot of

money for domain names. Compaq paid a small California software company $3 million for altavista.com. The owner of the domain name was a legitimate businessman. He had registered altavista.com in 1994. His company's name was Alta Vista. Of course he would want that domain name.

The owner of www.umbro.com had no such legitimate claim, however, and Umbro International Inc. refused to pay him. When Umbro, which markets soccer equipment, tried to register www.umbro.com, it found out that the name was already taken. Umbro demanded that the owner hand over the domain name. It included their trademark in the name, after all. The cybersquatter agreed—if Umbro paid fifty thousand dollars and promised a lifetime supply of Umbro soccer equipment.

Umbro took the cybersquatter to court. The judge told the cybersquatter to hand over umbro.com and to pay more than $23 million in legal fees. The cybersquatter had no money, so it looked like Umbro would not be able to collect the judgment.

Then Umbro went after Network Solutions, the company that had registered umbro.com. Umbro wanted Network Solutions to sell the cybersquatter's twenty-seven other domain names and turn over the money to the court. The sheriff could then auction off the domain names to the highest bidder. In February 1999, the court ruled in favor of Umbro. Network Solutions had to transfer the domain names into the court's control.[3]

That decision set a precedent that would define the rules of the domain name battle. Since then, most courts have ruled in favor of famous trademark owners. Fair use of a company's trademark on the Web is legal, the courts agree.[4] But using a company's trademarked name as a domain name and holding it hostage is not fair use.

Taxing the Net

Another important control issue is taxation. Americans have taken tax issues seriously since patriots used the slogan, "No taxation without representation" to rally colonists to break away from England. Americans still take the issue of taxation seriously.

In the mid–1990s, states, counties, and towns began eyeing the Internet and e-commerce as a source of tax money. Most states, counties, and towns depend on tax money to pay for community services, such as hospitals, police, and firefighters. In March 2000, for example, Governor Paul E. Patton said that Kentucky was losing about one third of its tax revenue because his state does not tax Internet sales.[5]

To make up the difference, some states levied a tax on Internet access charges. Internet access charges are what Internet service providers charge their customers for access to the Net. Some states passed Internet sales taxes. Some levied telecommunications taxes on users' Internet access. Some states taxed Internet sales. A few states taxed downloads of software, music, or data.

What Can Be Taxed?

Since the 1950s, states have been able to collect sales tax on catalog sales only if a company has a physical point of presence—or nexus—in that state. For example, Maine can charge sales tax on catalog items L.L. Bean sells to Maine residents because L.L. Bean has its corporate offices and its store in Maine. New Hampshire can charge its residents tax on L.L. Bean catalog purchases, too, because Concord has an L.L. Bean outlet.

Some states would like to extend the concept of nexus. The government of Connecticut decided in 1997 that having a modem in the state was enough

One issue that needs to be resolved is how states will tax sales at Internet stores.

to create nexus. It required America Online to add sales tax to the bills of its Connecticut customers. In 1997, Texas tax officials decided that downloading software from a server in Texas was no different from buying the software in Texas. If companies had a Web server in Texas, they had a nexus, and Texas could tax them. "If software is downloaded from a server here in Texas, then it's the same as coming to Texas to pick up the software even though you may be out of state," said Lindey Osborne, a state tax policy official.[6]

But taxing businesses is always a two-edged sword. Businesses create jobs. They help a state's economy. States that tax Internet access and sales will drive Internet-based businesses away. Companies will move to other states where taxes are lower, taking their business, jobs, and tax money with them. Cybersource, Inc., of San Jose, California, which sells software on the Internet, is one such company. Its president and CEO, Bill McKiernan, says that the Texas tax policy convinced him that his company needed to stay out of Texas if possible.[7]

Problems

Businesses, of course, opposed Internet taxes—and not only because they did not want to pay the money. With more than seven thousand tax jurisdictions across the nation, paying taxes could drive businesses out of e-sales altogether, companies complained. Just trying to obey seven thousand different rules could bury e-businesses under a mound of paperwork. And what would happen when more than one state, county, or city taxed a business on the same service or product?

Until someone can come up with a way to simplify Internet taxes, Congress is unlikely to change the tax law. In fact, in October 1998, Congress passed the Internet Tax Freedom Act, and President Clinton signed it into law. The new law imposed a moratorium of three years on Internet taxes. During that time, states agreed not to tax the Internet. The law also set up a commission to study the issue.

Of course, the federal government does not have the power to tell states what they can and cannot tax. No federal law could cancel the sales and Internet use taxes that states already had. No federal law could block the Internet-related taxes of Connecticut, North Dakota, South Dakota, Wisconsin, New Mexico, Tennessee, Ohio, and Iowa. Most states did agree to the moratorium, however. In 2000, as the end of the moratorium approached, the House of Representatives voted to extend the moratorium for another five years. The Senate, however, did not pass a similar bill, which means the extended moratorium was not passed into law.[8]

Tax-Free Zones

Even if states can tax the Internet, they may decide not to. It seems natural that companies will take their businesses to states that do not burden them with taxes. Hoping to lure Internet businesses to their states, California and Florida declared themselves tax-free zones.[9] That could change if state governments decide it is in their best interest to collect Internet taxes.

Consumers will decide with their pocketbooks. Barnes & Noble has its headquarters in New York, so New Yorkers have to pay an 8 percent sales tax on anything they buy from barnesandnoble.com. It is no surprise that Amazon.com, based in Seattle, gets 8.5 percent of its customers from New York, because they do not tax New York customers. Barnesandnoble.com gets fewer than 2 percent. Amazon has annual sales of more than $600 million. Barnesandnoble.com has some $60 million.[10] Clearly, online shoppers are savvy about ways to avoid paying sales tax.

The Future of Internet Taxation

Still, most businesses realize that taxing sales on the Internet, at least, is inevitable. State and local governments will not be able to lose tax money to Internet sales forever. But who will tax and how taxation will work is still a source of fierce debate.

Internet tax issues will continue to be a source of debate for years to come. So will the fight over domain names and cybersquatting. The wrangling over who is going to control the Internet will continue for a long time.

5

Privacy on the Internet

The Internet can be a dangerous place. "A criminal using tools and other information easily available over the Internet can operate in almost perfect anonymity,"[1] Deputy Attorney General Eric Holder told Congress in March 2000. Anonymous remailers are services that allow Internet users to send e-mail and surf the Web without anyone knowing who they are. Yet these free trial accounts help criminals get away scot-free.

Michael Vatis, director of the FBI's National Infrastructure Protection Center, says, "Individuals can hide or disguise

44

their tracks by manipulating logs and directing their attacks through networks in many countries before hitting their ultimate target."[2]

And Doug Rehman, president of the Florida Association of Computer Crime Investigators, comments: "In many ways, it's easier to commit crimes in cyberspace than in the real world. I don't think you're going to see law enforcement catch up with the curve."[3] Criminals can use the Internet to commit fraud and to trade child pornography. They can launder money by sending electronic cash anonymously. And there is nothing the police can do about it because the police do not know who the criminals are.

For example, in 1996, Georgia became the first state to pass a law that would have made it illegal to use a name that falsely identifies a speaker on the Internet. Less than a year later, the Northern District Court of Georgia struck the law down. This carelessly written law would have made it a crime to use any name other than a person's real name online. Children would have to use their real names online–which could be extremely dangerous. And even America Online screen names, the names millions of people use to identify themselves on the world's largest online community, would be illegal.[4]

A Not-So-Anonymous Threat

Michael Ian Campbell knows that people are not as anonymous on the Internet as they think. Two days before winter break 1999, someone calling himself

Soup81 contacted Columbine student Erin Walton via instant message on America Online. He warned her not to go to school the next day. He said he was going to finish what Eric Harris and Dylan Klebold started when they murdered twelve students and a teacher on April 20, 1999, before killing themselves. Scared, Erin begged him to say he was joking, but he did not.

After Soup81 signed off, Erin showed a copy of the instant message to her mother. Her mother called the sheriff, and Jefferson County authorities called in the FBI. Within twenty-four hours the FBI knew exactly who Soup81 was: eighteen-year-old Michael Ian Campbell.[5] Campbell pleaded guilty to one count of making a threat across state lines. In May 2000, he was sentenced to four months in prison.

Taking Cookies from Strangers

Not being able to make anonymous threats via the Internet is a good thing. But not being able to surf without nosy Webmasters collecting personal information worries a lot of people.

Web sites track the surfers who visit them. Web sites leave small electronic files of information on surfers' computers. These files are called cookies. Cookies can tell the owners of the Web sites what surfers like, what other sites they visit, how long they spend on each site, and what type of computer and browser they are using. Web sites use cookies to build a profile of each surfer who visits their site.

Most profiles may include general information—how many times the surfer has visited, what the

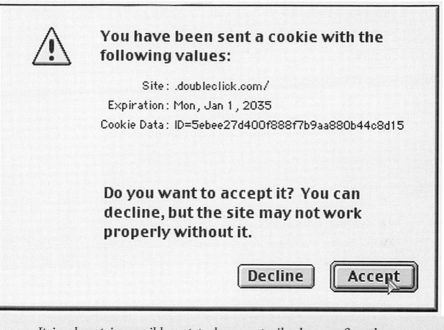

It is almost impossible not to leave a trail when surfing the Web. Many companies leave small electronic files of information called "cookies" on surfers' computers. Cookies can create a profile of the surfer (what he or she likes, or buys) for the Web site owner.

surfer is interested in, and what the surfer would like to buy. Web sites use these profiles to customize content for each user, to offer personalized customer service, and to target users with personalized advertising. There are two kinds of profiles: anonymous and self-reported.[6]

Simon started surfing the Web when he was twelve. One of his favorite sites is the Boston Red Sox official home page. He likes fast cars and skiing, and he reads a lot. His anonymous profile may look something like this.

ID#
Visited 6,420 times
Does not click on banner ads
Red Sox fan
Reads *The New York Times*
Looking for:
Jaguar
Harry Potter books

Next time Simon logs on to the site that placed this cookie on his computer, he may see a banner ad for sports cars. He may find a link to an online bookstore.

Simon often buys books from Amazon.com, so his Amazon.com profile is much more detailed and revealing. His self-reported profile may look something like this:

Simon
[unique identifying number]
1235 Street Avenue
Boston, MA
(XXX) XXX-XXXX
Mother's credit card: XXXX XXXX XXXX 1212
Bought:
Chicken Soup for the Teenage Soul
Harry Potter and the Goblet of Fire

As Simon continues to surf, his profiles will continue to fill up with more information about him.

Connecting the Dots

It used to be that only the site that placed the cookies on Simon's computer could read his cookies.

That changed when companies began to share the information they have collected. The biggest company was DoubleClick, which by the year 2000 had collected information from over ten thousand other sites. After DoubleClick, Simon's profile turned into a mega-profile, filled with data from more than one source. By the end of 1999, DoubleClick had more than ten thousand online partners and 100 million cookies, chock-full of information.

It did not take long for DoubleClick to connect the dots and learn the name and address of the surfer who liked Jaguars, skiing, and the Red Sox. Simon had to register at many of the sites he visited, so those sites knew who he was. DoubleClick had long ago planted a cookie on Simon's hard drive. DoubleClick sent the cookie's ID number on to some of the sites Simon visited. If any one of those sites sent back information in Simon's self-reported profile, DoubleClick could put a name to the Red Sox fan who dreamed of owning a Jaguar.

Of course, people who do not want to be identified can refuse to sign up for any site that demands personal information. But for Simon it was too late. Chances are, he had no idea what DoubleClick was up to. He had probably never even heard of DoubleClick.

Privacy activists had heard of DoubleClick, however, and they did not like it. Some objected to compiling click-by-click profiles without a user's knowledge or permission.[7] Others objected because users had no idea exactly what information each cookie stored.

Companies now exist solely to share the information collected by "cookies." DoubleClick is the biggest such organization.

Most surfers, however, did not worry too much about DoubleClick. From the beginning, DoubleClick promised that the information it collected would be safe. The company would never give it away or sell it.[8]

Double Cross

DoubleClick's Privacy Policy in 1998 read: "All users who receive an ad targeted by DoubleClick's technology remain completely anonymous. We do not sell or rent any information to third parties. Because of our efforts to keep users anonymous, the information DoubleClick has is useful only across sites using the DoubleClick technology and only in the context of ad selection."

Then DoubleClick joined Abacus Direct

Corporation, which had a database of more than 88 million detailed buyer profiles collected from records of over 2 billion catalog purchasing transactions. That information included consumer names, addresses, phone numbers, e-mail addresses, and "click data."[9]

In June 1999, DoubleClick changed its privacy policy. The company would, in fact, share the information it had collected with DoubleClick's advertisers and Web publishers.[10]

Privacy watchdogs were furious. Their anger was heightened by the fact that DoubleClick refused to say which Internet sites were passing on registration information. Why did the company refuse? DoubleClick's partners would not like it if the company gave out their private information without permission, DoubleClick vice president Jonathan Shapiro said.[11]

Jason Catlett of Junkbusters, a privacy watchdog site, called DoubleClick's refusal "a shameful hypocrisy." DoubleClick had no right to protect the privacy "of the violators of privacy. . . . For four years [DoubleClick has] said they don't identify you personally, and now they're admitting they are going to identify you."[12]

Opt In? Opt Out?

Not so, Shapiro said. Users who do not want to be tracked can opt out. All they have to do is fill out a form saying that they do not want a Web site to collect information on them. But opting out is not that easy. Surfers might have to opt out at all the sites they visit. And privacy statements are usually long and hard to understand. They may also be hard to find.

In July 2000, DoubleClick's privacy statement ran to more than two thousand words in small type. DoubleClick's opt-out option ran three pages into its Web site, and it would not work unless a surfer accepted the site's cookies first.

The opt-out hyperlink was in small type in a navigation box toward the end of the right-hand column—below links for investor relations, careers at DoubleClick, a Pricewaterhouse-Coopers audit report, the customer support center, and the learning center.[13]

Few surfers know that they can choose to opt out, activists say. Failing to opt out is not the same as actively giving permission.

Privacy activists complained to the Federal Trade Commission (FTC). The Electronic Privacy Information Center filed a lawsuit. Rather than face an uncertain judgment, DoubleClick backed off for the time being. But one thing is sure: Privacy activists continue to watch the situation closely.

Following the Cookie Crumbs

In July 2000, DoubleClick was delivering over 30 billion ads for clients every month and collecting information on most surfers who passed through one of the company's client sites. Simon was one of those surfers. DoubleClick and other companies knew what

Simon had bought on the Internet. They knew what he had looked at but did not buy. They knew how long he spent at each DoubleClick-affiliated site he visited. DoubleClick, privacy activists charged, had turned the Web into a surveillance tool.

Companies like DoubleClick could pass on Simon's information to the government, insurance companies, and employers. If Simon's mother visited a Web site about cancer, her insurance company might find out. If Simon's father surfed job-search boards, his boss might be able to find out. And someone might use the information DoubleClick stored in his profile to blackmail his family.

In response to a complaint from the Electronic Privacy Information Center, the Federal Trade Commission opened an investigation into DoubleClick's practices. The FTC called for the industry to regulate itself in privacy issues, but the agency also asked Congress for the authority to protect consumers and to establish standards for using and selling consumers' personal data.

Government Surveillance

Even as Congress considered passing laws to protect Americans' privacy online, the FBI and other agencies worried that child pornographers, drug dealers, and money launderers could hide behind the Internet's shield of anonymity. Law enforcement agencies took advantage of the new technology to snoop on more and more Americans.

Echelon is the National Security Agency's automated monitoring system. It captures satellite, microwave, cellular, and fiber-optic traffic. The NSA is only allowed to collect information on foreign citizens. It is not allowed to gather information on Americans. However, technology has blurred the distinction. Echelon scoops up communications to and from North America.[14]

The FBI's FIDNet, Federal Intrusion Detection Network, monitors computers that connect to government computers. Privacy watchdog groups charged that checking on the status of a citizen's income-tax refund or Social Security record could trigger government red flags and investigations of innocent citizens. And there was no guarantee the FBI would delete the information they collected, even if there was no evidence of a crime.[15]

The Communications Assistance for Law Enforcement Act, passed in 1999, required the communications industry to include snooping capabilities in telephones. The Justice Department also asked Congress for the authority to secretly break into homes and offices to obtain decryption keys or passwords or to modify computers so that law enforcement could read encrypted, or coded, messages or files. That part of the bill was dropped, however.[16]

In April 2000, the FBI asked Congress for $75 million to develop a better surveillance system. Digital Storm is a multimedia system of computers that can sift through data from a variety of sources and link what they find to create profiles of individuals.[17]

And in the summer of 2000, Americans learned of the FBI's e-mail surveillance tool, Carnivore. Carnivore is software that scans and captures "packets," the standard unit of Internet traffic. The FBI could install a Carnivore unit on the Internet service of someone under investigation. Privacy groups complained that Carnivore violated the Fourth Amendment's protection against unreasonable search and seizure.

The American Civil Liberties Union went to court to force the FBI to turn over everything about the program, including technical specifications, documentation, and even the actual programming code. Even as a judge ordered the FBI to set a time-line for turning over the information the ACLU requested, the House Judiciary Subcommittee on the Constitution heard public testimony on Carnivore.

As Americans become more and more dependent on electronic communications, both big business and the government will continue to find new and better ways to snoop on the communications of the average citizen.[18] Internet users have a well-connected network of privacy watchdogs, however, which will keep a wary eye on the government and make any new snooping device public as soon as possible.

Fighting Back

Internet users also have other means to defeat those who would invade their digital privacy. A number of online companies have sprung up to let users surf anonymously. Zero-Knowledge Systems' privacy software, Freedom 1.0, hit the Web in December 1999.[19] Freedom 1.0 uses strong encryption to scramble the information into a secret code. It also reroutes users through a number of servers around the world. That makes it harder for anyone to trace the source of the communication.

Another privacy site is Anonymizer.[20] Anonymizer lets surfers look like they are using a different server from the one they really are. Anonymizer also filters cookies. By the year 2000, both popular browsers, Netscape and Internet Explorer, also allowed Web surfer customers to filter cookies, site by site. Some Web sites will not work without cookies. Surfers have to enable cookies or avoid those sites.

The battle over online privacy is far from over. It will continue to be fought in the halls of Congress, in the courts, and on the Internet.

6

Encryption

The first computers were invented during World War II to do one job: create and break secret code. The very existence of the automated computing machines was top secret. The machines were huge and expensive.

No one could have foreseen that one day millions of people would own their own personal computers. No one could have imagined desktop, laptop, and note-book computers. And no one could have ever dreamed that the Internet would one day connect computers around the world. No one could have guessed that one day businesses would use e-mail to share company secrets. They could not have known that people would send credit card information over the Internet.

During World War II, encryption was a weapon of war. So were the machines that generated the secret codes. In fact, apart from the atom bomb, there was no weapon more important than the work of the code breakers, or cryptographers, and their machines. Many historians agree that Britain's cryptographers saved millions of lives and probably shortened the war by two years.[1]

How Encryption Works

Cryptography is the science of turning information into gibberish called cyphertext. Only someone who has the key—or "decoder ring"—can read the message. Today, software can do the work of cryptography. Some encryption programs are longer than others. Their strength depends on the length of their keys. Computer generated encryption keys are measured in bits. The more bits a key has, the stronger the encryption is. Forty-bit encryption, which was the U.S. government standard for many years, has 72 quadrillion possible combinations.

Until about thirty years ago, there was only one kind of secret code, single key encryption. With single key encryption, both the writer of a message and the reader have to use the same key to encode and decode messages.

That creates a problem. Communicating the "key" in the mail or by telegraph or telephone would not be very secure. Someone could intercept a letter or telegram. Someone could eavesdrop on a telephone conversation. During World War II, key couriers traveled with satchels handcuffed to their wrists. It was a dangerous mission. There was always the risk that an enemy would put a gun to the courier's head and demand the key to the code. Both sides knew that the information in those satchels was more valuable than bombs.[2]

Today's encryption—public key encryption—no longer requires the communication of a secret key. Instead, it works with two keys, a public key and a private key. A computer generates both keys. The public key is like a telephone number. People list their public keys in directories, put them at the end of e-mails, and pass them along to friends. Owners of private keys keep them secret. They use the private key to decode anything that has been encrypted using their public key.

With public key encryption, people who have never met before can communicate privately without worrying about someone intercepting the secret decoder ring. Public key encryption is also important because it guarantees that the sender of the message is who he says he is. For example, if someone wants to withdraw money from an online bank, the bank wants to know for sure who it is dealing with.

Cracking the Code

Of course, encryption is not perfect. Code can be broken. Someone who wants to break a code can apply brute force. An example of using brute force is figuring out an ATM number by starting with 0000 and trying every number up to 9999. Most codes have more than ten thousand possibilities, however. Often it is easier to find a weakness in the code and take advantage of that.

Today's public key encryption is much more sophisticated than anything spies had during World War II. But so are the ways of breaking code. Today it is possible to crack 40-bit encryption in just hours. That is why many Americans, especially those concerned about their privacy on the Internet, wanted access to 56-bit and even stronger encryption programs.

Pretty Good Privacy

During World War II, the United States had learned that cryptography could be a powerful weapon. The government declared that all encryption devices were weapons of war. Americans could not export encryption devices without the permission of the State Department. This was not a problem until personal computers and the Internet became popular. Once that happened, people wanted to know that their electronic communication was secure.

In 1991, Phillip Zimmermann, a software consultant, believed that Congress was about to make it illegal for private citizens to use strong encryption. He knew something had to be done before a law could be passed. If private citizens across the United States already had access to a

Philip Zimmermann, a software consultant, feared that the U.S. Congress was going to make it illegal for citizens to use strong encryption. He created a nearly uncrackable code, which someone posted on the Internet.

strong computer encryption program, it would be harder for Congress to stop it. Zimmermann decided it was up to him. He wrote a nearly uncrackable encryption program. He called it Pretty Good Privacy, PGP for short, and he gave it away to anyone who wanted it.

The law that would have kept Americans from using strong encryption was never passed. But there were still laws against exporting it. The State Department had limited the export of encryption programs with keys longer than forty bits. Forty-bit keys are too short to use for military purposes. And that is where Phillip Zimmermann got into trouble. Someone posted PGP to the Internet, and soon it had spread from Australia to Mongolia.[3]

Suddenly everyone was talking about encryption. The Justice Department labeled Zimmermann an international arms trafficker. He faced the possiblility of serving more than four years in prison. His legal bills grew to more than one hundred thousand dollars, but privacy rights activists rallied around him. They paid his lawyers and publicized his plight on the Internet. The Justice Department dropped the case in January 1996.[4]

The Debate

Meanwhile, the military and law enforcement wanted to continue to ban the export of encryption stronger than forty bits. The military and the FBI worried about encryption in the hands of international terrorists.

Computer software companies complained that controls on the export of encryption were hurting their business. Besides, did the government think that foreign cryptographers could not come up with their own strong code?[5] Average citizens complained that they needed strong encryption too—to protect credit card numbers and medical records, trade secrets and personal communication—especially on the Internet.[6] Yes, it was true that strong encryption could be used to commit crimes. But so could tire irons. There were no laws controlling the export of tire irons.

Congress listened. Some legislators suggested a law that would relax export restrictions, but no such law was passed. The Clinton administration agreed with the military and law enforcement. In 1993, President Clinton tried out a new idea on the American people—the Clipper chip. The Clipper chip was a tiny silicone chip that would be installed in all telephones and computers that used encryption. The chip would have a back door, and the government would have a key to that back door. With a court order, police could use the key to decode any encrypted messages stored on a computer or listen in on encrypted telephone conversations.

The response was immediate and deafening. To privacy watchdogs, it looked like another case of the government trampling constitutional rights. The First Amendment protects Americans' right to free speech. The Fourth Amendment protects Americans from unreasonable search and seizure of their private possessions. But the federal government wanted a way to snoop on all Americans' telephone conversations. Why not require all Americans to hand over copies of the keys to their cars and homes, privacy groups asked.

Americans did not trust the government to honor their privacy—and for good reason. The government had used information they had collected about private citizens to lock Americans of Japanese ancestry in concentration camps during World War II. The first director of the FBI, J. Edgar Hoover, had illegally snooped on Martin Luther King, Jr., in the 1960s. And President Nixon had spied on the enemies of his administration.

Many people agreed with author Solveig Singleton, who wrote:

> Government poses a unique and special danger to privacy because only government has the power to control the armies, the police, and the courts. So the Constitution of the United States carefully limits the powers

of the government; the Bill of Rights restricts the power of the police to snoop without a warrant.[7]

The Clinton Administration could see that the American people would not accept the Clipper chip. After a year of silence, the administration tried again. Clipper II would have the same back door, but a responsible third party would hold the key. The government would snoop only when absolutely necessary.

Americans said no again. A 1995 Gallup poll found that more than half of Americans believed their government had become so large and powerful that it posed a threat to the rights and freedoms of ordinary people.

A year later, the Clinton administration tried again. The administration would relax export controls on strong encryption if the government was allowed to hold the keys to encryption programs stronger than 56 bits. This time it was not only the American people who rejected the idea. In April 1997, the European Commission called for the use of strong encryption as a "foundation stone of electronic commerce."[8] In August of that same year, a federal district court judge ruled that encryption export controls were unconstitutional. In 1999, France, Britain, and Germany publicly rejected the Clinton Administration's latest plan. And U.S. companies that sold encryption software simply moved to countries that did not control the export of oncryption.[9]

By mid–1999, the Clinton Administration gave

up. In January 2000, the White House announced new regulations. While the new regulations did not drop controls altogether, they did make it easier for companies and average citizens to export strong encryption software.

It was the need for privacy on the Internet that drove the debate over encryption. It was the voices of millions of netizens around the world that forced the most powerful government in the world to rethink its position in the debate. Debates on other Internet issues will probably be decided in much the same way.

7

Online Copyright and Information Theft

In March 2000, author Stephen King and publisher Simon & Schuster released the first exclusively e-book, *Riding the Bullet*. For $2.50, netizens could download an encrypted copy of the ten-thousand-word novella. The software for reading e-books was free.

The experiment was a huge success—except for one thing. Stephen King could not read his own book even if he paid the $2.50. King found himself in the same predicament as Jon Johansen, a Norwegian teen who could not watch the DVDs he bought on his Linux computer.

King owned a Macintosh, and only Microsoft Windows users could read his new e-book.

Within days hackers broke the encryption and posted the text on the Internet for anyone to download.

Warez

As soon as companies began selling software separately from hardware, computer owners began stealing it. In the early days, many companies built copy protection into their software. In order to play "Where in the World Is Carmen Sandiego?" early users had to insert the program disk in the floppy drive.

Almost immediately, software crackers learned to disable the protection and make copies of their games for their friends. At first they traded warez—software that has been stripped of its copy protection and made available for illegal downloading—over local bulletin boards. Then, as more and more people logged onto the Net, warez pirates set up Web sites and used newsgroups to trade. The pirates are still at it today.

Software piracy is illegal. It is theft, and most pirates know that. Nevertheless, it is easy for them to rationalize what they are doing. Many argue that pirating warez is not stealing. "If I steal your dog, then I've got your dog and you don't," one pirate said, "That's theft. But we're not taking anything away from anyone. [Jailed hacker] Kevin Mitnick didn't steal those credit card numbers. He just copied them. They're still sitting back where he found them."[1]

Many pirates argue that they should be able to copy software freely because "information wants to be free."[2] Early Internet guru Stewart Brand wrote in 1987: "Information wants to be free because it has become so cheap to distribute, copy and recombine. . . . It wants to be expensive because it can be immeasurably valuable to the recipient." Internet pirates have conveniently forgotten about the second part of Brand's statement. Richard Stallman, a spokesman for the Free Software Foundation, argues that sharing information can only make humanity richer.[3] In his online writing, Stallman expands on his argument: "Cooperation is more important than copyright," he says, and "You deserve free software."[4]

Software companies claim that piracy deprives software programmers of fair compensation. If programmers do not get paid, they argue, no one will program software. Pirates laugh at that notion and point to the high cost of software as an excuse for pirating software. "How rich does Bill Gates have to be?" one pirate asked. And Stallman points out that programming is fun. In the early days of personal computers, they did it for free, he says. People who like to program will continue to do so whether or not they get rich from programming.[5]

Law enforcement and software companies do not accept any of those arguments. The FBI's Computer Crime Squad prosecutes nationwide software piracy rings as well as individual software pirates.

And the Software Publishers Association (SPA) and the Business Software Alliance (BSA) take piracy very seriously Piracy, they say, does more than hurt individual programmers. It puts software companies out of business and workers out of jobs. It contributes to rising software costs. Both the SPA and the BSA are aggressive about bringing civil lawsuits against warez traders.

Teen warez traders may not deprive software companies of much income. Most could not afford the software they copy and trade, and they would not buy it. For many teen traders, piracy is more about trophy collecting than actually using the illegal software. Adults, however, do cost software companies money. And the problem is worldwide.

Illegal software accounts for 25 to 50 percent of the software in use in the United States. And the problem is worse in other countries. For example, AutoCAD, a very expensive design program, has a 90 percent share of the computer-aided design market in China. But almost every copy of AutoCAD in China is pirated.[6]

In the United States, pirates are most often teen boys. In Malaysia and much of Southeast Asia, however, crime syndicates run computer piracy rings. In 1998, almost three quarters of software used in Malaysia was pirated. And Malaysia is not the worst offender. Vietnam tops the list, with only 3 percent of all software being legal in 1998, followed by China and Indonesia. Oman, Lebanon, the countries of the former Soviet Union, and Bulgaria complete the list of top offenders.[7]

Fighting Back

In 1997, Congress passed the No Electronic Theft Act, and the FBI has used the law to step up prosecution of online pirates. Eric John Thornton was one of them. The twenty-four-year-old offered free software on his Web site. Thousands came, clicked, and downloaded—until 1999, when the FBI came, shut down the site, and seized all of Eric's computer equipment. In December 1999, Eric pleaded guilty to electronic theft. Shortly after his plea, his Web site was back up with a new message, which stayed online for eighteen months.

The software companies began to fight piracy in new ways. They used television public service announcements to compare illegal downloading of software to shoplifting packaged software from a store. They also audited corporations they believed were using illegal software. Many companies paid big fines.

But software companies will find that there is no rest in the battle against piracy. The Internet has made copying software and other digital material too easy for some people to pass up. People who are dishonest in the real world will be dishonest in cyberspace. But the software companies and the government have raised awareness of the issue. Pirates can no longer claim they did not know trading warez was illegal.

Evil House of Cheat

Another problem the Internet has contributed to is cheating in school. The same technology that has made it easy to pirate software also makes it easy for students to plagiarize copy the work of others and pass it off as their own.

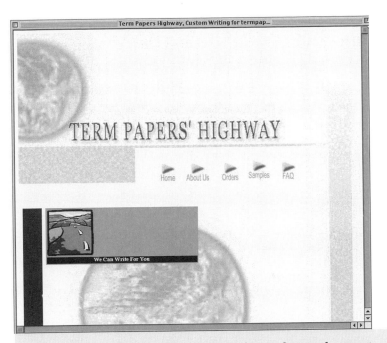

The Internet has proved a bonanza for students who want help on their term papers and tests. Some sites exist that specifically help with term papers, while others simply contain essays written by other students, which can be downloaded for free.

Erin Carlson had no idea how much trouble her Web site would cause when she started it in 1996. At first, she posted a couple of her own essays. Then students across the country started e-mailing copies of their own writing to add to her site. By 1999, almost a million people had visited her Web site. Erin suspected some students were plagiarizing the essays posted on her site, but no one had complained to her about it.

One day, the dean of her university called her into

his office. He said he had received fifty calls about her Web site from upset teachers. Most of them wanted the university to kick her out. Erin was shocked. No one had complained to her. Erin knew that the First Amendment protected her site, whether the teachers liked it or not. She kept the site going for a while but discontinued it shortly before its millionth hit.

The response was swift. Students around the world begged her to put the site back up. A student named Kim wrote: "I do not understand the difference between your site and *Cliff's Notes*. Maybe I am missing the point as I am not a teacher but I feel reading someone else's take on a subject helps to enhance learning much like a study group." Another student, Morphius, wrote: "I have copied some of your work, or plagurised [sic], and I have no qualms about it. Plagurism [sic] existed before the net. Plagurism [sic] will always exist and taking down one site wont [sic] stop me at all."[8]

"Download Your Workload"

Dozens of sites sell school assignments on the Internet. Some give papers away for free. But the popularity of cheat sites is not the fault of the Internet.

A recent survey conducted by *Who's Who Among American High School Students* indicated that cheating is common. Eighty percent of high-achieving high school students admitted to having cheated at least once. Half did not believe cheating was wrong all the time. And 95 percent of the cheaters had never been caught. Other studies showed that college students had similar attitudes toward cheating.[9]

Fifty years ago, the statistics were much different. Then, only about 20 percent of college students admitted they cheated in high school. Today more than 75 percent of college students admit that they cheated in high school.[10]

Students throughout the ages have turned to plagiarism to lighten their load. Internet technology, however, has made cheating easier than ever before in history. Honor students and future dropouts alike head to the Internet for plagiarized essays.

Some students are fuzzy about the difference between research and plagiarism, and it is no wonder. The rules are not clear. Many schools stress teamwork and cooperative learning. Some ambitious parents "help" turn out sophisticated science projects. Some guidance counselors help students get into exclusive colleges by guiding the words and information students include in their college application essays. And some teachers help their students cheat on standardized tests.

But many students do not need the help of an adult. Technology offers a wealth of choices for cheating. Aside from the term-paper mills, the Internet offers chat rooms where students swap science projects and instant messages with the answers to a math homework assignment. Students can share e-mail complete with test questions between classes, and some hack into school computers to alter their transcripts and the transcripts of their friends. Students can use cell phones to send the answers to multiple-choice tests to friends' pagers. Palm computers and high-tech calculators can store math formulas and historical dates.

Plagiarism and Copyright Infringement

It is not only young people who steal other people's intellectual property. In 1994, a Danish researcher found one of his own papers on the U.S. National Library of Medicine site, Medline. But he was not listed as the author. Another person, Andrzej Jendryczko, had plagiarized the paper and put his own name on it. A search of Medline showed that Jendryczko had plagiarized another twenty-nine papers.[11] Naturally, Jendryczko's reputation was ruined. No one would trust anything he wrote ever again.

Pretending to be the author of another person's writing is plagiarism. Plagiarism is not only dishonest; in many cases, it is also against the law. In most countries around the world, writers have the right to decide how their creations will be used. That right is called copyright. Andrzej Jendryczko had not only plagiarized Marek Wrontildeski's work. He had also infringed on his copyright.

Creative work is valuable. No one wants to paint a portrait, write a poem, or compose a song just to have someone else steal it and make money from it. Copyright law guarantees writers and artists the right to make a profit from their own creative work or intellectual property. The creator of a work is the only person who can legally sell, lease, or give someone else permission to use the work. Copyright law protects both published and unpublished works.[12] Trademark law protects against fraud. Nike's trademark guarantees that Nike shoes are really Nike shoes, for example.

In 1998, President Clinton signed the Digital Millennium Copyright Act into law. Under that law, copyright and trademark owners can sue people who infringe on their rights. The law also made it a crime to break software copy protection and to make, sell, or distribute software to help others illegally copy software. People who did infringe on copyright for financial gain could go to prison for between five and ten years and be fined from five hundred thousand to one million dollars.[13]

Software companies hoped that the new law would give them some relief from the pirates. At the time, the music industry barely noticed the problems software companies were having. That industry would soon find itself under attack from a whole new generation of music pirates.

8

Music Pirates

Justin Frankel was sixteen when he won his first programming contest at the University of Northern Arizona in 1995. But Justin was not interested only in programming. He was a big music fan, too.

In 1987, the German engineering firm, Fraunhofer Schaltungen, invented a new way to compress digital audio files. It was mpeg-1 Audio Layer 3, MP3 for short. MP3 compresses huge CD-quality sound files into packages that are tiny enough to send across the Internet.

As download speeds got faster, MP3 caught on. In the mid–1990s, college students started exploring the world of free digital music. Justin Frankel was one of those students. He liked downloading and listening to music, but he did not like the way he had to do it. At that time MP3 players were clunky. So Justin decided to build a better MP3 player. By April 1997, WinAmp was done. Justin uploaded it to the Web.

A New Way to Listen to Music

WinAmp looks like a home stereo. It can jack up the sound quality with 3-D surround sound and reverb. Like most physical CD jukeboxes, WinAmp can sort tunes or play them randomly. It is reliable and easy to use. As an added bonus, music fans could download WinAmp "skins" from the Internet, pictures that let them customize the MP3 player to look exactly the way they wanted it to look. WinAmp was shareware—software that people can try out before they buy. After using the software for a trial period, users can register and pay for the software or delete it from their systems.

Justin asked for a ten dollar registration fee. During WinAmp's first month, forty thousand visitors visited Justin's Web site every day. A year and a half later, 15 million people had downloaded WinAmp. The registrations started rolling in. There was more money from companies that advertised on his Web site— about eight thousand dollars a month. When Justin turned twenty-one, he was worth about $70 million.

For many college students, WinAmp was a dream come true. Trading of MP3s took off, swamping university computer networks. A lot of musicians loved WinAmp, too. They started to believe there might be a way out of their dependence on the recording labels.

Panic Time for the Recording Industry

The once all-powerful Record Industry Association of America (RIAA) was at risk. People who were using WinAmp and the other clones that quickly sprang up were sharing—not buying—music. Young people were buying a third less music than ten years before. RIAA's monopoly was beginning to crumble. Two million copies of *NSYNC's *No Strings Attached* sold in its first week on the market in March 2000. That same week, someone illegally posted the entire album on the Web. Over one million fans downloaded the album without paying a cent for it.[1]

Music industry enforcers trolled the Web for pirates, people who were downloading copyrighted music without paying. They took Diamond Multimedia to court, trying to stop the manufacture of the MP3 player Rio.

Music industry enforcers trolled the Web for pirates, people who were downloading copyrighted music without paying.

The palm-sized Rio brought music fans the kind of sound quality they might expect from a CD player. But owners could upload whatever songs they wanted from their computer. No more having to play a whole CD just to listen to one song. Rio was bound to be a winner. The RIAA claimed that Rio would promote music piracy. But the judge disagreed. He ruled against RIAA. Rio was no different from cassette recorders and VCRs. Rio and other MP3 players hit the stores.[2]

MP3 Wars

On the Internet, MP3.com and Napster Web sites let users listen to digital music from their personal collection via any computer connected to the Internet. Music fans could also keep an online MP3 catalog of the music in their CD collection. They could also listen to existing digital music from MP3.com bands, songs from existing CDs, and new CDs purchased from MP3.com online retail partners. Thousands of music fans found copyrighted music at MP3.com and downloaded it without paying for it.

The RIAA sued MP3.com for making unauthorized copies of forty-five thousand audio CDs, loading the unauthorized copies onto file servers, and letting its users listen to and download those unauthorized copies. MP3.com and Napster should not be allowed to create a way for fans to find and download hundreds of thousands of music files without paying, the record industry said. Artists deserve to be paid for their work. So do their labels.

Napster Inc. founder Shawn Fanning at a news conference in San Francisco, after a ruling that Napster must stop its free Internet-based service from sharing copyright material.

MP3.com and Napster argued that they did not store music files at their sites. The RIAA was trying to punish the technology, rather than the lawbreakers.[3] MP3.com and Napster are like copy machines, they said. No one expected the Xerox company to control what users copied with its machines. Many copy machines come with signs warning users not to break copyright laws. So did MP3.com and Napster. And Napster's rules were even more stringent than the rules posted for copy machine use.

Backlash

In the midst of the MP3 and Napster lawsuits, the Federal Communications Commission came down on the recording industry for having inflated CD prices since 1995. Few music fans felt sorry for the record companies because they agreed.

The artists were a different story. "Nobody likes to work for free, and that is what Napster was forcing artists to do," said Scott Stapp of Creed. "Napster is sneaking in the back door and robbing me blind."[4] Some people did feel sorry for the artists.

Other fans were not impressed, especially after Metallica and Dr. Dre filed lawsuits of their own and threatened to go after individual students who had downloaded their music illegally. Huge numbers of fans turned on Metallica and Dr. Dre. An anonymous music fan expressed the feelings of many at Time Digital's message center: "yoou [sic] know what i think? i think these guys aare [sic] . . . cheap . . . , i mean give me a break, they're . . . millionaires . . . what . . . are they gonna do with more money!!!"[5]

A number of musicians also sided with MP3.com and other music-sharing sites. Some went so far as to break ranks with the studios and distribute their music directly on the Internet.[6] Rapper Ice-T released an album on the Internet and liked the control he had over his own music. He also liked not having to give most of his profit to the recording industry. "File sharing is one of the coolest things on the Internet," Ice-T told ZDNet Music. "Napster might be the enemy of the labels, but not of the musicians."[7]

U.S. District Judge Jed Rakoff, however, sided with the RIAA. He ruled against MP3.com[8] and in mid 2001, Napster was still fighting for its existence in court. However, in many ways, it did not matter how many battles the RIAA won. It had already lost the war. Digital music was not going away.[9] A whole generation had grown up getting things for free on the Internet. For them, copyright law and thirty-minute download times seemed trivial.

Already Gnutella and other file-swapping networks had hit the Web. Gnutella had no central Web site. The program allowed Internet users to set

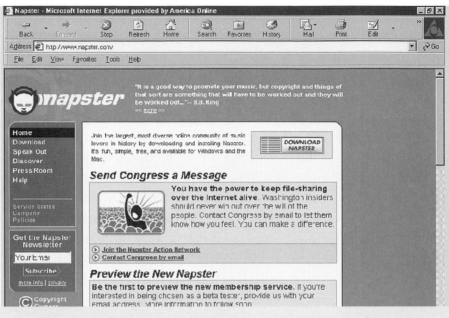

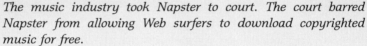

The music industry took Napster to court. The court barred Napster from allowing Web surfers to download copyrighted music for free.

aside a part of their hard drive for storing files. Other Internet users could use Gnutella to find and download files. With Gnutella each computer could become a Napster or an MP3.com. It would be much harder to control Gnutella and its users. What is worse for copyright is the fact that Gnutella and similar software let users trade much more than music—text documents, audio, video, and software.

The music industry would have to go after Gnutella music pirates one at a time. Prosecuting them in court would be cumbersome and expensive, if not impossible. The recording industry was going to have to come up with a new way to do business.

The Industry Wises Up?

If the record industry had not been so busy fighting the new technology, it might have realized that the best way to stop music piracy was to cash in on the MP3 trend. That is what other businesses had done. In 1999, Amazon.com watched free Sarah McLachlan digital downloads send advance sales of the album through the roof. So Amazon.com started offering more free promotional downloads.[10]

But all the music industry could see was that its monopoly over the distribution of music was slipping away. They decided that creating their own download and playback technology would control piracy. In August 2000, the Secure Digital Music Initiative (SDMI), a group of technology and recording companies, came up with a "pay-per-listen" scheme.

A "persistent protection" code would stay with the music file as well as any copies. The owner of a CD or digital music file could let anyone in the world copy the music, and it would be legal. That is because anyone who wanted to listen would have to pay with a credit card first.[11]

WinAmp's creator, Justin Frankel, does not believe that technology will ever completely stop music piracy. Listeners will be able to capture the digital stream and turn it into an MP3 file. And there is always someone who will be able to crack the protection. Still, music lovers may find that paying a dollar or so to download the tunes they want is easier than pirating them.[12]

DVD Spillover

In January 2000, Norwegian police arrested Jon Johansen, a sixteen-year-old hacker, for cracking the Content Scrambling System (CSS) for DVDs and distributing the DVD cracking software over the Internet. Sites carrying the program were shut down. And the Motion Picture Association of America, which represents the major Hollywood studios, filed a lawsuit against him.

Jon could not understand why. Yes, he cracked DVD's copy protection, but he was no DVD pirate. He only wanted to play the CDs and DVDs he had paid for. At the time, CSS did not work on his computer's operating system, Linux. He reverse-engineered the copy-protection code. His software, which he called DeCSS, let him watch his DVDs on computers that did not use the Windows operating system.

The Digital Millenium Copyright Law—the law used to prosecute Jon—allows people to reverse engineer software to make a product operate on another computer platform. Furthermore, the international agreement on intellectual property, the Berne Convention on Copyright, allows consumers the right of "fair use." Fair use permits copies for personal use and for backup. It is legal to copy a CD to a cassette tape or a DVD movie to VHS tape. Certainly it should allow Jon to watch his own DVDs.

Suddenly Jon was a worldwide celebrity. Major computer companies offered him jobs because of his obvious programming talent. The Electronic Freedom Foundation (EFF) offered to help the Johansen family find lawyers to defend Jon in court.[13] Many Net users felt the Hollywood studios had targeted Jon unjustly and posted his recipe for DeCSS on their Web sites, and Eric Corley published the code in his online magazine, *Hacker Magazine 2600*.[14]

The Motion Picture Association of America immediately filed suit for copyright infringement. Corley argued that the First Amendment protection of free speech guaranteed his right to publish the code. In August 2000, U.S. District Judge Lewis A. Kaplan ruled that the MPAA's computer code was a trade secret, not speech. Source code, he said, was different from speech.

Copyleft, an online computer-related clothing company, had been contributing to the EFF's legal fund by selling OpenDVD t-shirts with the source code for DeCCS printed on the back. The DVD Copy Control Association went after Copyleft.[15] The Association said that the DeCSS source code was not protected by the First Amendment and that Copyleft had no right to print the DeCSS source code on its shirts.

In August 2000, a New York U.S. district court ordered the publisher of *Hacker Magazine 2600* to stop publishing or linking to other Web sites that offer the DeCSS program. Joseph Wecker protested by writing a song, *DVDdescramble.c*, which puts DeCSS code to music. He posted the MP3 version of his song on the Internet.[16] In January 2001, a number of interested associations joined with the American Civil Liberties Union to ask a federal appeals court to overturn the August 2000 ruling.[17]

That same month, Internet service provider Verio joined the fight. One of its customers posted a court document that contained the movie industry's CSS code. The court sealed the document after it went up on the Web, but Verio refused to force the customer to take the information off his site.[18]

But Carnegie Mellon Professor David Touretzky pointed out that being able to print the recipe for DeCSS on a shirt makes it obvious that the legal wrangling is more about speech than about trade secrets. "If you can put it on a t-shirt," he testified in Corley's trial, "it's speech." EFF lawyers expected that the Supreme Court would eventually decide the cases.[19]

The debate over the legality of DeCSS will not decide the larger debate over copyright and intellectual property. It will probably take years for netizens, companies, the courts, and lawmakers to iron out what copyright should mean on the Internet.

9

Hackers

Mike (not his real name—under federal law, juvenile defendants are not named) and some of his friends were in. They had hacked into the Worcester, Massachusetts, telephone company computer. They decided to look around the network. In the process, they crashed the computer they had hacked into. The crash shut off telephone service to Worcester Regional Airport for six hours. Air traffic control was disrupted. Six hundred homes also went dark.

The U.S. Secret Service investigated. They caught the teens and prosecuted Mike, the ringleader. Under the terms of his plea bargain, Mike was sentenced to two years' probation, a five thousand dollar fine, and two hundred fifty hours of community service. During his probation, he was not allowed to use any computer with a modem.[1]

Mike was the first teen to be prosecuted by the federal government for the commission of a computer crime.[2] That was in 1998. Mike was fourteen. Since then, the Justice Department has gone after a number of teens for computer hacking. U.S. Attorney Donald K. Stern states, "Computer and telephone networks are not toys for the entertainment of teenagers. Hacking a computer or telephone network can create a tremendous risk to the public and we will prosecute."

Mike and his friends did not mean to cause any damage. Like many teen hackers, they did not think of what they were doing as a crime. The government, however, did see it as a crime. Fed up with a rash of youthful hackers bragging about their exploits, the Justice Department began to prosecute the young offenders.

The Earliest Computer Hackers

The earliest hackers were students at the Massachusetts Institute of Technology (MIT) in the 1960s. MIT had the first large computer networks. The students worked on a large mainframe computer, learning to program and pushing computer technology to its limits. They also began to link computers to form networks. Then they explored the networks to learn everything about how they worked. These hackers did not steal or destroy. They explored and created. They were members of a tiny technological elite.

As computer students linked to one another via nationwide networks, MIT's hacker culture took hold. Hackers shared their exploits and their discoveries. They continued to push technology to its limits. And they made important discoveries that improved the way computers and networks operated.

Phreakers: Telephone Hackers

Even before the Internet, there were hackers. They were fascinated with the telephone system. They wanted to know how it worked. Nothing would keep them from finding out. They were called phreakers.

Phreakers focused on tricking the telephone company's electronic equipment into connecting long-distance calls for free. Some phreakers studied university level telephone communications textbooks. Some—known as dumpster divers—sorted through telephone company dumpsters at night, looking for old manuals, computer code, and passwords. Others sweet-talked telephone company employees into giving them privileged information.

Still others learned by experimenting. Joe Engressia was blind from birth, but he had a talent that made him a very good phreaker. He could remember any musical note he heard and whistle it exactly. As a young boy, he learned he could make free long-distance calls by whistling certain tones.[3]

John T. Draper—aka Captain Crunch—was another

early phone phreaker. In 1972, he accidentally learned that the toy whistle in a box of Captain Crunch cereal made a sound that would let him make long-distance phone calls. Captain Crunch was also famous for routing a long-distance phone call through seven countries around the world and then back to himself. After a twenty-second delay, he would hear his own voice.

At first, phreaking was an honorable pastime. Exploring was good, phreakers agreed, but wholesale stealing of telephone service was not. In fact, members of the Mafia asked Captain Crunch to put his phreaking skills to work for them. He refused and was beaten badly.[4]

However, as the secret of phreaking got out, less honorable phreakers took over. They made free long-distance calls. They billed calls to fake credit cards or to large corporations. They thought their actions were harmless. They did not damage the telephone company. The cables were there. Why not use them? The telephone companies did not see it that way, however. They tracked phreakers down and had them prosecuted.[5]

Recreational Hackers

When microcomputers first moved from huge rooms to offices and homes, many phreakers turned away from the telephone company in favor of computers. They used some of the same methods they had used as phreakers to expand their computer skills. They prided themselves on their knowledge of computers and really wanted to learn. Some built their own computers from kits. Others wrote software. Still others hooked their computers up to telephone lines and explored far distant networks.

Some early hackers are still well known today. Steve Wozniak and Steve Jobs built computers in a garage and pushed the technology to see how far it would go. They went on to found Apple Computer. Bill Gates, founder of Microsoft, was also an early hacker.

Crackers: Criminal Hackers

Not all the early hackers were so benign. The first hackers the public heard about were two teenagers whose hacking nearly plunged the world into thermonuclear war in the movie *War Games*. Fortunately, those hackers were fiction.

The members of the 414 gang were real people. In 1983 they broke into the computer system of a New York cancer hospital and accidentally destroyed data. News stories about the incident made the term hacker a household word—a very negative word.

Other hackers specialize in getting into computers and networks where they do not belong. Network hackers may dial thousands of phone numbers, hoping to hear the screech of a computer connection. Once they find a computer, most hackers try to get root access or complete control over the system.

To crack (break) into a computer network, says a computer expert who goes by the name Nirgenwo, a hacker has to trick a remote computer into believing that he is someone the computer knows and trusts. User names and passwords help computers tell the difference between a hacker and the system administrator. However, war dialer programs can try thousands of passwords until one is right. And often people use passwords that are easy to guess.

Cracking a computer goes something like this:

People who hack into computer systems can destroy a company's, or a nation's, hard drive. Imagine how many people might be harmed if someone hacked into a hospital's computer system.

Computer: Hello.

Hacker: Hi, I'd like to come in and look around.

Computer: Hold on a minute. Who do you think you are?

Hacker: (lying) I'm the system administrator.

Computer: What's the password?

Hacker: (types in the password)

Computer: (opening the door) Come in.

Once hackers have root access, they can steal private information, delete files, or crash the system. Some cover their tracks or build back doors that they can enter again later.[6]

Most of the time, hackers break into computer systems just to prove that they can. Then they head for chat rooms and online bulletin boards to brag. Sophisticated hackers leave no trace of their activities. Other hackers, however, cause serious damage.

In February 2000, hackers unleashed denial of service attacks on Yahoo!, e-Bay, Amazon, CNN, and other prominent sites. Denial of service attacks flood a network with fake requests or millions of nonsense messages. The network is so busy dealing with the attacks that it cannot perform its regular jobs. If there are enough messages, the network will shut down altogether. Experts estimated that losses from the attacks added up to millions of dollars.[7]

Barely a month later, two Welsh hackers used the Internet to commit a more traditional crime: robbery and extortion. They broke into e-commerce sites and stole credit card information from over twenty-six thousand accounts. They threatened to publish the credit card numbers on the Internet unless the owners of the Web sites paid them off. This kind of computer crime is easy to identify and prosecute. Robbery and extortion are crimes, whether or not criminals use computers to commit them.[8]

It was much harder to prosecute several Filipino students who released the Love Bug virus in May 2000. The deadly virus spread around the world in record time. A virus is a small program that sneaks into a computer system via the Internet or infected software. Some viruses are harmless. Others destroy data and shut down computers. The Love Bug virus was hidden in a small file called "I love you." When a user downloaded the file, the Love Bug destroyed some sound and graphics files. Then it spread itself via e-mail to the first fifty addresses in the computer's address book. The virus shut down computer networks around the world and cost companies millions for the time their employees could not use their computer networks.[9]

Script Kiddies

By the late 1990s, when hordes of young people took up hacking, learning to crack computers and create viruses was much easier than ever before. The Internet-wide hacker population jumped from about thirty-five thousand in 1998 to one hundred thousand in the year 2000, according to the Information Security Advisory Group.[10] The FBI's caseload jumped from 547 to 1,154 computer intrusion cases between 1998 and 1999. And businesses were reporting more attacks, as well.[11]

The newbies—people just starting out as hackers—could find ready-made hacking programs on thousands of Web sites worldwide. Hacking had become a sport in which almost anyone could participate. The problem with that was that the new breed of hackers did not have the skills of the early hackers, who regarded them with contempt. Real hackers called this new group of clueless amateurs script kiddies.

Generally young and male, some members of Internet gangs defaced Web pages with digital graffiti.[12] Others unleashed the programs they downloaded without a clue about what those programs might do. They caused damage they had no idea how to reverse. The hacker cult hero who goes by the name SirDistic dismissed the person who attacked Yahoo! with contempt: "You are not a hacker," he wrote in an open letter on America Online, "and you do not deserve respect for your childish actions.

Frequently changing passwords makes it harder for hackers to crack the system.

You are no better than the twisted individuals who spray a crowd of innocent bystanders with a machine gun, only to nick your intended target."[13]

Government vs. Hackers

Law enforcement investigators learned quickly that even if they could not track hackers electronically, they could usually find them in chat rooms. Script kiddies, it seemed, could not resist the urge to brag about their exploits.

For Attorney General Janet Reno, all hackers were criminals, and she put them on notice. The Department of Justice would go after computer criminals, she warned.

The attorney general was not kidding. In 1999, the FBI tracked down Ehud Tenebaum after he broke into computers at the Pentagon and commercial and educational institutions. Ehud fled to Israel, but Israeli national police placed him under house arrest.[14] Chad Davis, whose alias was Mindphasr, was sentenced to six months in prison for cracking the U.S. Army's Web site. He was also ordered to pay more than eight thousand dollars in restitution.[15] And nineteen-year-old Eric Burns, whose alias was Zyklon, was sentenced to fifteen months in jail for defacing the White House Web site.[16]

In 2000, Montreal police arrested Mafiaboy, age seventeen, for the February denial-of-service attacks that shut down Yahoo!, CNN, and other high-profile Web sites.[17] The same year, Max Vision, also known as Max Ray Butler, was indicted for breaking into

NASA, the Department of Defense, and other government systems.[18]

Lords of the Files

Today, ironically, Internet security companies are turning to former hackers to help secure their computer systems. In 1998, the seven Boston hackers known as LOpht Heavy Industries bragged to Congress that they could shut down the Internet "in 30 minutes."[19] Today they are members of a successful computer security consulting firm, @Stake.

The former members of LOpht are no script kiddies. They know computers inside out. They know from experience that most computer systems and software are unprotected. And today they use the hacker tools they themselves created as teens to protect computer networks.

Ironically, these former teen hackers will have to deal with a large and increasingly sophisticated group of hackers as well as the inferior script kiddies. Jeff Schiller, who is in charge of computer security at the Massachusetts Institute of Technology in Boston, says, "Any 14-year-old can break into your computer these days if it's attached to a phone."[20] It will be up to the grown-up hackers to rein in the fourteen-year-olds.

10

The Dark Side of the Internet

The Internet is an exciting world for most teens. It has made things possible that today's parents and grandparents could never have dreamed of when they were in school. But the Internet also has its dark side. Most teens know how to handle themselves online, but some get burned.

Spam and Scams

Make $50,000 in 90 days!
Meet babes!
Work at home. Make millions.
Lose weight.
You have won a cruise!

Spam is junk e-mail that Internet users did not ask for. Spam is not usually dangerous, but it is annoying. Spammers buy huge lists of Internet addresses. They send out their junk e-mails to all those addresses with the click of a mouse.

America Online reports that up to 30 percent of the e-mail it processes is spam.[1] Spam wastes electronic resources and irritates netizens. AOL and other service providers filter spam. Of course, spammers can often find a way around the filters. Some use forged e-mail addresses and innocent-sounding subject headings. Others move their online accounts from provider to provider. By the time a filter can block them out, they have moved on.

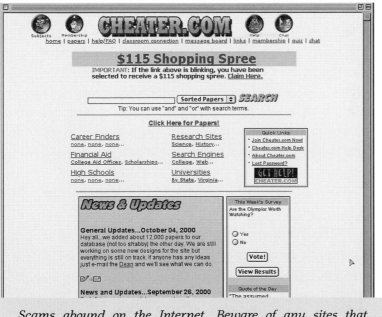

Scams abound on the Internet. Beware of any sites that promise something for nothing—especially cash.

Many spam e-mails are invitations to visit pornographic sites. Most are rip-offs or scams. The spams that are most likely to disturb children and young teens are those that pretend to offer something young people want. When the child clicks on "Free Beanie Babies," for example, she finds herself looking at pictures of people having sex.

Most online services are doing everything they can to stop spam. However, the most effective thing children and teens can do about spam is never to respond to it or forward it to another user. It is best to delete spam immediately, without even opening the e-mail if possible.

Internet Addiction

Cyberspace can help teens explore the world and find independence. It can be an escape, or a place to vent, act out, or cry for help. Some teens may become addicted.

Perhaps the most famous claim of Internet addiction came from Michael Ian Campbell. His online threats to finish the job Eric Harris and Dylan Klebold had started shut down Columbine High School in Littleton, Colorado, for two days. He later withdrew the claim that he was addicted to the Internet.

The diagnosis of Internet addiction began as one psychiatrist's joke. But other members of the psychological community thought he was onto something. Dr. Kimberly Young, who studies and treats Internet addiction, has started her own practice on the Web. That may seem strange, but Dr. Young says that the Web is the best place to find and treat Internet addicts.

Not all teens are susceptible to Internet addiction, she says, any more than all teens who drink are in danger of becoming alcoholics. Some will always be casual users, and some may go through phases of intense Internet use. Teens most likely to become addicted are those who have to deal with serious problems in their real lives. Those are the teens most likely to use the Internet as a way to avoid dealing with their problems.

The signs of Internet addiction are similar to the signs of any addiction. Internet addicts will deny that there is a problem. They are likely to lie about how much time they spend online or about what they are doing while they are on the computer. Many Internet addicts lose sleep in order to spend more time online. They may neglect to bathe or forget to eat. Their grades may drop. Many Internet addicts withdraw from real life. They drop their real-life friends and activities and spend all their time with online friends and activities. If their parents cut them off from the computer or restrict their time online, Internet addicts may become withdrawn or angry.

Hate.com

Many believed the Internet would bring peace and tolerance to the world. The Internet's reach would help people to get to know and understand one another. That understanding would erase fear, prejudice, and hate. Unfortunately, the opposite has sometimes happened. The Internet has become a home to hate groups waiting to snare the unwary surfer. In the past, it was not easy for hate groups to contact other people with similar beliefs. On the Internet, extremists have created an electronic community of hate.

Today, extremists can communicate easily in cyberspace. They reinforce one another in their hateful beliefs. Members of hate groups can come together in newsgroups, chat rooms, and private e-mail groups. They can communicate anonymously with encrypted e-mail. But their favorite forum is the Web. In newsgroups and chat rooms, other members can disagree with them or make fun of their beliefs. On the Web, hate groups can control the content and refuse to publish anything that contradicts their beliefs.

Many hate groups target African Americans, Asians, Jews, and other minorities. Others focus on homosexuals, abortion rights supporters, and the U.S. government. The First Amendment protects hate speech on the Internet, as it does in books, pamphlets, and newspapers.

What worries Howard Berkowitz, national chair of the Anti-Defamation League, is that many hate sites use appealing propaganda and attractive multimedia to try to draw in young people. One site offers children crossword puzzles and pages to color. Other sites target teens with "bigotry-laced hard rock."[2]

Furthermore, some groups go out of their way to make their sites look like mainstream sites. For example, one Aryan hate site used Web addresses that people expected would take them to the Web sites of large, popular newspapers. Instead Web surfers found themselves reading hate propaganda. Worried about their reputations, the newspapers took legal action to stop that practice.

Hate groups will not go away. It is virtually impossible—legally or technologically—to regulate speech on the Internet. However, when Internet hate groups incite violence or libel, harass, or threaten other citizens, the First Amendment does not protect them. For example, when a young man sent death threats to sixty Asian-American students at the University of California, Irvine, in 1998, he was sentenced to a year in prison.

An anti-abortion Web site called "Nuremburg Files" posted photos, names, addresses, and license plate numbers of abortion doctors. Three doctors were murdered. After each one died, the site owner drew a line through his name. Planned Parenthood, several doctors, and one abortion clinic filed suit against the nationwide American Coalition of Life Advocates and the Portland, Oregon, based group, Advocates for Life Ministries, in federal court in 1995. Their suit claimed that the Web site incited violence against abortionists and their patients in violation of the 1994 Clinic Entrances Act. A Portland jury found that although the Nuremberg Files Web site did not explicitly call on people to murder the doctors, the information it posted constituted a real threat of bodily harm. The anti-abortion activists on trial were ordered to pay over $100 million in fines.[3] In March 2001, the Ninth U.S. Circuit Court of Appeals reversed the ruling.

Pornography

There are hundreds of thousands of porn sites on the Web. Young people can innocently mistype a Web address and find themselves looking at pictures they find disgusting or disturbing. Others click on hyperlinks in e-mail or other Web pages and find themselves trapped in Web sites that will not let them escape. Clicking the browser's back button only leads to more hard-core pictures. The only way to escape is to log off, and sometimes even that is impossible. Web surfers may have to force their computers to shut down.

Online pornography has become a billion dollar business. And it is a business that is not going away. Most online porn is protected by the First Amendment. Child pornography, however, is not protected, and law enforcement agencies across the country are going after online child pornographers.

In 1995, the FBI discovered that pedophiles were using the Internet to lure children into danger and to trade child pornography. The Bureau created a new division, Innocent Images, to track down child pornographers online. Some detectives went undercover in chat rooms, posing as adults looking for pornography. Once they find someone who is offering illegal pornographic images, they arrest the person. They also pose as teenagers in order to catch and arrest adults who are willing to travel to have sex with children and teens. It is a federal offense to cross a state line in order to have sex with a minor.

In 1999, Innocent Images averaged 124 cases a week.[4]

Predators

Aggressive investigations have put some child pornographers and child predators behind bars. But there seems to be an endless supply of them on the Internet. Predators spend a lot of time in chat rooms, looking for innocent teens to lure into meeting them for sex. Those predators put young lives in jeopardy.

Melinda (not her real name) was sixteen and living in New Mexico when she met Brian E. Rolfs in the Wizard's Realm, an Internet chat room popular with teens. She chatted with him online for a time. Melinda liked Brian enough to accept his offer to fly her to Missouri, where he lived.

When she reached St. Louis, Melinda found out that her Internet dream date was instead a nightmare. Brian picked her up at the airport, took her home, and raped her. The next day, he gave her $250 for airfare and left her at the airport. Melinda flew back home and called Albuquerque police.

In court, his lawyer argued that Bryan E. Rolfs, twenty-four, was not a predator but a confused kid. The jury disagreed. In July 1998, Bryan was fined three thousand dollars and sentenced to prison for fifteen months. After he got out of prison, Rolfs spent three years on supervised release. During that time, he was not allowed to have computer equipment without the permission of probation officials, had to get psychological therapy, and stay away from people younger than seventeen.[5]

The Statistics

No one knows how many children and teens are approached by pedophiles on the Internet. Usually authorities only learn what has been going on in the aftermath of a tragedy. At the beginning of 2000, police were investigating as many as eight hundred cases of adults and children meeting on the Internet and then traveling to meet for sex, according to the Crimes Against Children Research Center survey.[6]

A serious problem on the Internet is the number of people who prey on children. At the beginning of 2000, law enforcement agencies were investigating eight hundred cases of adults meeting children online and traveling to meet them for sex.

Less dramatic Internet contacts include unwelcome requests for sex, both online and in real time, and also e-mail and instant messages that include pictures that make children and teens uncomfortable. The Online Victimization survey found that one in five children aged ten to seventeen who use the Internet regularly, has been solicited for sex. In one in thirty-three cases, an online predator has asked to meet, called on the telephone, or sent gifts or money in the mail.[7]

Seventy-five percent of the teens surveyed ignored the harassment. They left the site, logged off, or blocked the harasser. But pre-teens, especially, found the incidents disturbing.[8] It is the needy, troubled teens who make the best targets. One convicted child molester told a reporter that he pretended he was seventeen. He attracted teens by making them feel loved. He pretended to care about them and to understand what they were going through. "Once you get their confidence," he said, "it's easy to manipulate them."[9]

On the Trail of the Predators

Julie Posey is a Colorado mother who hunts down online predators. Pretending to be a thirteen-year-old, she logs onto AOL and heads for a chat room. It usually only takes minutes for the instant messages to start popping up. "Are you alone?" some ask. "What are you wearing?"

Mrs. Posey had learned a lot in her first four years as an online predator hunter. Sometimes she would get sixty instant messages in three minutes.

Some predators send their victims prepaid phone cards so that their real-life contact will not show up on their parent's phone bill. Others send disposable cameras. They ask their victims to take pictures of themselves and mail the camera back.

Mrs. Posey has seen a lot, too. One predator, who had already been arrested once for molesting a child, told her to wear spandex to their meeting. "Spandex to me is like kryptonite to Superman," he wrote. Another predator, about to be released from a halfway house, was on the hunt even before his probation was approved. He went back to jail for four years. And then there was the man Posey met online one Monday. On Thursday, he hopped in his car and drove five hundred miles to meet her. Police were waiting for him when he got to the park where they had agreed to meet. As of July 2000, Julie Posey had participated in nineteen arrests.[10]

Detective James McLaughlin of Keene, New Hampshire, also surfs the Net for predators. He worries that children and teens give away too much personal information online. Several years ago, McLaughlin joined a chat room where kids from Keene liked to hang out. Eighty percent of the young people revealed enough about themselves that he could easily find out exactly who they were, using public records, like the telephone book. And if Detective McLaughlin could do it, so could a predator.[11]

Who are the predators? According to the Online Victimization survey, about two thirds were male, and about half were teens themselves. In 20 percent of cases, the predators were between eighteen and twenty-five years old, with 4 percent being older. In other cases, the victim had no idea how old the predator was. Most predators—65 percent—find their victims in chat rooms. Another 24 percent meet via instant message.[12]

Keeping Secrets

One of the most disturbing findings of the study was that only about half of the children and teens told anyone that they had run into trouble online. They did not tell their parents or even their friends.[13]

It is true that many parents are behind the curve technologically. But there are also many adults— teachers, ministers, counselors, family friends, and older brothers and sisters—who are Net savvy and will know how to get help.

11

Looking Ahead

"Suppose all the information stored on computers everywhere were linked. Suppose I could program my computer to create a space in which anything could be linked to anything."[1] When Tim Berners-Lee had that idea some twenty years ago, he did not envision a technical toy. He dreamed of using technology to help people around the world work together. He could not have dreamed that his vision would literally change the world.

He may have had some idea of the issues that his World Wide Web would raise. After all, the issues surrounding the Internet and World Wide Web are the same ones that people have always had to deal with. They are control, trust, privacy, and the gulf between rich and poor.[2]

Those core issues will always be the core issues. New questions will arise as society finds its way in the netted and webbed world. As humans work them out, they will create a media sensation for awhile and then slip into history.

The Internet was designed to survive a nuclear war. It will survive debates over censorship, cybersquatting, piracy, and encryption. It will survive hackers, pirates, pornographers, haters, and pedophiles. It will even survive governments' efforts to control it.

The public Internet—the World Wide Web—is entering its teen years now. Like any teen, it is finding its way. It is growing at warp speed.

As people learn to live with this wonderful, young technology, new issues will continue to surface. Some of the challenges discussed in this book may have already been resolved. Some will become more contentious.

One thing is sure. The Internet will continue to provide a rich source of debate for years to come.

Chapter Notes

Chapter 1. A Little Bit of History

1. Tim Berners-Lee, *Weaving the Web* (San Francisco: HarperSanFrancisco, 1999), p. 4.

2. Ibid., p. 22.

3. Scot Finnie, "Twenty Questions: How the Web Works," CNET Coverage, August 28, 1997, <http://coeage. cnet.com/Content/Features/Techno/Networks/ss03.html> (June 22, 2000).

4. Marguerite Holloway, "Molding the Web," *Scientific American*, December 1997, <http://www.sciam.com/ 1297issue/1297profile.html> (June 21, 2000).

5. Berners-Lee, p. 125.

Chapter 2. The Digital Divide: Falling Through the (Inter)Net

1. Betty Reid, "Getting iMac to Girl Tough on Reservation," *The Arizona Republic*, March 1, 2000, <http:// www.azcentral.com/news/0301imac.shtml> (April 28, 2000).

2. Steve Crouthamel, "The Navajo People," *Desert USA*, 1996–2000, <http://www.desertusa.com/ind1/du_peo_ navjo.html> (June 2, 2000).

3. Jill Lawrence and Richard Benedetto, "Clinton Works for Net Access for Native Americans," *USA Today*, April 17, 2000, p. 14A.

4. Scott Andrews, "Digital Divide in East Palo Alto," April 16, 2000, <http://dailynews.yahoo.com/h/ap/ 20000416/tc/tale_of_two_cities_1.html> (April 17, 2000).

5. Terence Hunt, "Clinton Addresses Shiprock Crowd," *Albuquerque Journal*, April 17, 2000, p. 1.

6. Palo Alto Unified School District, *State of the District Report, 1999–2000*, February 2000, <http://www.pausd. paloalto.ca.us/district/district.html> (July 7, 2000).

7. Fiber to the Home (FTTH) Trial, city of Palo Alto, March 15, 2000, <http://www.city.paloalto.ca.us/utilities/ fth> (August 2, 2000).

8. Kevin Galvin, "Clinton Moves to Close the Internet Gap," *The Seattle Times*, April 17, 2000, <http://www.seattletimes.com/news/natioworld/html98/digi17m_20000417.html> (April 17, 2000).

9. Lawrence and Benedetto, p. 14A.

10. *Falling Through the Net: Defining the Digital Divide: A Report on the Telecommunications and Information Technology Gap in America*, Washington, D.C.: U.S. Department of Commerce, National Telecommunications and Information Administration, November 1999, <http://www.ntia.doc.gov/ntiahome/fttn99/FTTN.pdf> (April 17, 2000), p. 83.

11. "The Clinton-Gore Administration: Outlining America's Agenda For The Information Age," *White House at Work*, March 3, 2000, <http://www.ciao.gov/press_ release.htm> (February 12, 2001).

12. Lawrence and Benedetto, p. 14A.

13. Robert J. Eiserle, "Small Tax with Large Consequences," *The Record* (Bergen County, N.J.), September 27, 1999, p. l02.

14. Randall E. Stross, "Digital Divide Hooey," *U.S. News and World Report*, April 17, 2000, p. 45.

15. Galvin.

16. "How Many Online?" *NUA Internet Surveys*, 2000, <http://www.nua.net/surveys/how_many_online/index.html> (February 11, 2001).

17. Janet Black, "Losing Ground Bit by Bit," *BBC News*, BBC Online Network, November 1, 1999, <http://news.bbc.co.uk/hi/english/special_report/199/10/99/information_rich_information_poor/newsid_472000/472621.stm> (April 18, 2000).

18. *Bridging the Digital Divide in Central and Eastern Europe*, Global Internet Liberty Campaign, March 2000, p. 12.

19. Anthony Faiola and Stephen Buckley, "Poor in Latin America Embrace Net's Promise," *The Washington Post*, July 9, 2000, p. A1.

20. "Bridging the Digital Divide," *BBC News*, BBC Online Network, October 14, 1999, <http://news.bbc.co.uk/hi/english/special_report/1999/10/99/information_rich_information_poor/newsid_466000/466651.stm> (April 18, 2000).

21. Sakiko Fukuda-Parr, Richard Jolly, et al., *Human Development Report 2000*, United Nations Development Program, p. 197.

22. *Human Development Report 2000*, United Nations Development Programme, 2000, p. 197, <http://www.undp. org/hdr2000/english/HDR2000.html> (June 20, 2000).

23. Black.

24. Ibid.

Chapter 3. Censoring the Internet

1. David Case, "Big Brother Is Alive and Well in Vietnam—And He Really Hates the Web," *Wired*, November 1997, <www.wired.com/wired/archive/5.1/es_vietnam_pr. html> (May 28, 2000).

2. Patrick Symes, "Che is Dead," *Wired*, February 1998, <www.wired.com/wired/archive/6.02/cuba_pr.html> (May 28, 2000).

3. Case.

4. "Library Net Filter Proposal Defeated," *USA Today*, February 12, 2000, <http://www.usatoday.com/life/cyber/ tech/cth425.htm> (May 28, 2000).

5. *Peacefire Page*, 1996–2000, <http://peacefire.org> (August 25, 2000).

6. Internet Wiretap Server, December 10, 1997, <wiretap. area.com> (February 11, 2001).

7. UEN Log Files, September 10–October 10, 1998.

8. Christopher Morley, *The Haunted Bookshop*, 1919, Classical Literature Library, <http://www.authorslibrary. net/b/hbook10.htm> (August 26, 2000).

9. Michael Sims, et al., "Censored Internet Access in Utah Public Schools and Libraries," *The Censorware Project Page,* March 1999, <http://www.censorware.org/reports/ utah/conclusion.shtml> (August 26, 2000).

10. Reid Goldsborough, "On the Net, Speak Freely But Think First," *Techweek*, September 7, 1999, <http://www. techweek.com/articles/9-7-99/help.htm> (June 9, 2000).

11. "First Amendment Protection Extended to the Internet," *Minneapolis Star Tribune*, June 27, 1997, p. 1A.

12. Michelle V. Rafter, "Hope High For Free Speech On 'Net," *St. Louis Post-Dispatch*, June 26, 1996, p. 8C.

13. Ibid.

14. "First Amendment Protection Extended to the Internet," *Minneapolis Star Tribune*, June 27, 1997, p. 1A.

15. "Expletives Undeleted," *St. Louis Post Dispatch*, December 30, 1998, p. B6.

•••

16. "Court Upholds Expulsion of Student for Web Site," *Student Press Law Center News Flash*, July 18, 2000, <http://www.splc.org/newsflashes/071800pennsylvania.html> (July 22, 2000).

17. Robyn Blumner, "Censorship Goes Beyond the Gates," *Denver Rocky Mountain News*, September 18, 1998, p. 49A.

18. Deborah Mathis, "When Does School Safety Become Oppression?" Gannett News Service, June 14, 1999, p. ARC.

Chapter 4. Who Controls the Internet?

1. Jeremy Quittner, "The Lemonade Stand Circa 2000: A Boy, a Site, a $10 Million Lawsuit," *Business Week*, January 6, 2000, <http://www.concentric.net/~Franatty/BusWeek.htm> (July 29, 2001).

2. Rosalind Resnick, "Departments & Columns: 101 Domain Names: Is Deregulating the Answer?" *Netguide*, June 1, 1997, p. 57.

3. Carl S. Kaplan, "With Ruling, Internet Enters the Domain of Property Law," *Minneapolis Star Tribune*, April 18, 1999, p. 4D.

4. Mike Fimea, "Cyber Cases Heat Up: Scottsdale Firms Lose Web Site," *The Arizona Republic*, February 24, 2000, p. 1.

5. "Taxing Internet Sales Levels the Playing Field," *Business Week Online*, March 27, 2000, <http://www.businessweek.com/2000/00_13/b367487.htm> (April 18, 2000).

6. Patrick Thibodeau, "Welcome to www.you-owe-tax.com," *Computerworld*, June 16, 1997, p. 1.

7. Ibid.

8. "House Passes Extension of Net Tax Moratorium," *The Dallas Morning News*, May 11, 2000, p. 2D.

9. "Internet Taxation Questions and Answers," *CyberTax Channel*, 2000, <http://www.vertexinc.com/taxcybrary20/CyberTax_Channel/q_n_a_77.asp> (July 12, 2000).

10. James T. Madore, "Shoppers, Governments in Dispute Over Issue of Online Sales Tax," *Newsday*, August 15, 1999, p. F6.

Chapter 5. Privacy on the Internet

1. Declan McCullagh, "U.S. Wants Less Web Anonymity," *Wired News*, March 1, 2000, <http://www.wired.com/news/politics/0,1283,34659,00.html> (July 1, 2000).

2. Michael A. Vatis, "Internet Security," Congressional Testimony, March 7, 2000.

3. Troy Wolverton and Greg Sandoval, "Net Crime Poses Challenge To Authorities," *CNET News.com*, October 12, 1999, <http://news.cnet.com/news/0-1007-200-850601. html> (July 1, 2000).

4. The Georgia Computer Systems Protection Act, 1996, is available on the Internet at <http://www.clark. net/pub/rothman/gacode.htm> The court case, American Civil Liberties Union of Georgia, et al., v. Zell Miller, 1996, is available at <http://www.efga.org/hb1630/index.htm>. The order of the United States District Court, Northern District of Georgia, Atlanta Division, finding the Georgia Internet law unconstitutional, June 22, 1997, is available at <http://www.aclu.org/court/aclugavmiller.html> (July 5, 2000).

5. "Florida Teen Is Arrested," *ABCNews.com*, December 17, 1999, <http://abcnews.go.com/sections/ us/DailyNews/columbine991217.html> (June 1, 2000).

6. "Understanding Online Privacy," *The Privacy Page*, 2000, <http://www.myprivacy.org/privacy_index.htm> (June 22, 2000).

7. Viktor Mayer-Schonberger, "The Internet and Privacy Legislation: Cookies for a Treat?" *West Virginia Journal of Law and Technology*, March 17, 1997.

8. Mark E. Fogle, "Christmas Cookies Anyone?" *Web Review*, December 20, 1996, n.p.

9. Will Rodger, "Activists Charge Doubleclick Double-Cross," *USAToday*, <http://www.usatoday.com/life/cyber/ tech/cth211.htm> (June 8, 2000).

10. Sarah Lai Stirland, "Privacy Advocates Decry Doubleclick," Redherring.com, January 31, 2000, <http://www.redherring.com/investor/2000/0131/ invdclick013100.html> (August 25, 2000).

11. Rodger.

12. Ibid.

13. *DoubleClick Home Page*, 1996–2000, <http://www. doubleclick.com> (July 4, 2000).

14. Memorandum on Internal Electronic Surveillance Center for Democracy and Technology, June 7, 1999, <http:// www.cdt.org/digi_tele/echelon_signon.html> (July 1, 2000).

••

15. Michael J. O'Neil and James X. Dempsey, "Critical Infrastructure Protection: Threats to Privacy and Other Civil Liberties and Concerns with Government Mandates on Industry," Center for Democracy and Technology, February 10, 2000, <http://www.cdt.org/security/fidnet/oneildempseymemo.hmtl> (July 4, 2000).

16. "Justice Department Proposes Secret Searches of Homes, Offices," CDT Policy Post, The Center for Democracy and Technology, August 20, 1999, <http://www.cdt.org/publications/pp_5.19.html> (August 26, 2000).

17. Robert O'Harrow Jr., "Digital Storm Brews at FBI," *The Washington Post*, April 6, 2000, p. A1.

18. "Taps, Traps, and Pens—Electronic Surveillance Overview," *Center for Democracy and Technology Page*, July 4, 2000, <http://www.cdt.org/digi_tele/tapstraps.shtml> (July 4, 2000).

19. *ZeroKnowledge Page*, n.d., <http://www.zeroknowledge.com> (August 25, 2000).

20. *Anonymizer.com Page*, 2000, <http://www.anonymizer.com> (August 25, 2000).

Chapter 6. Encryption

1. "Decoding Nazi Secrets," NOVA, Public Broadcasting System, November 9, 1999.

2. Philip Zimmermann, Testimony to House Subcommittee for Economic Policy, Trade and the Environment, U.S. House of Representatives, October 12, 1993, available on the Electronic Freedom Foundation Web site, <http://www.eff.org/pub/Privacy/Crypto_export/zimmermann_export_101293.testimony> (June 10, 2000).

3. Scott Woolley, "Banned in Washington," *Forbes Magazine*, April 21, 1997, p. 162.

4. Steven Levy, "Cypher Wars: Pretty Good Privacy Gets Pretty Legal," Wired.com, November 1994, <http://www.wired.com/wired/archive/2.11/cypher.wars_pr.html> (June 23, 2000).

5. "Decoding Nazi Secrets."

6. Solveig Singleton, *Cato Handbook for Congress* (Washington, D.C.: The Cato Institute, 1998), p. 193, <http://www.cato.org/pubs/handbook/hb106/hb10619.pdf> (February 12, 2001).

7. ———, "Can You Trust the Ministry of Privacy?" *Today's Commentary*, August 25, 1998.

8. "Milestones, 1997 to Present," Center for Democracy and Technology, 2000, <http://www.cdt.org/crypto/milestones.shtml> (July 22, 2000).

9. Ibid.

Chapter 7. Online Copyright and Information Theft

1. David Pogue, "Some Warez Over the Rainbow," *MacWorld*, October 1, 1997, p. 190.

2. Tim Hamlin, "Piracy . . . Let's Be Honest!" GamersUniverse Productions, June 27, 1998, <http://www.gamersuniverse.com/piracy.html> (May 23, 2000).

3. Dorothy E. Denning, "Concerning Hackers who Break into Computer Systems," Proceedings of the Thirteenth National Computer Security Conference, Washington, D.C., October 1990, <http://www.cs.georgetown.edu/~denning/hackers/HackersNCSC.text> (July 22, 2000).

4. Richard Stallman, "Why Software Should Not Have Owners," Free Software Foundation, Inc., May 31, 2000, <http://www.gnu.org/philosophy/why-free.html> (June 20, 2000).

5. Ibid.

6. David M. Stone, "Software Piracy," University Laboratory High School, Urbana, Ilinois, February 12, 1999, <http://lrs.ed.uiuc.edu/wp/crime/d-stone2/piracy.html> (April 21, 2000).

7. Maryanne Jones Thompson, "BSA/SPA Global Software Piracy Report," *The Standard*, July 10, 1998, <http://www.thestandard.com/research/metrics/display/0,2799,9975,00.html> (April 22, 2000).

8. "If You Plan To Plagiarize An Essay Off The Web . . ." n.d., <http://www.elee.calpoly.edu/~ercarlso/warning.html> (August 26, 2000).

9. Carolyn Kleiner and Mary Lord, "The Cheating Game," *U.S. News & World Report*, November 22, 1999, <http://www.usnews.com/usnews/issue/991122/cheating.htm> (February 11, 2001).

10. "Teen Cheating Hurts All," *USA Today*, November 9, 1998, p. 24A.

11. Eliot Marshall, "Scientific Misconduct: The Internet: A Powerful Tool for Plagiarism Sleuths," *Science*, January 23, 1998.

12. "Copyright Basics," U.S. Copyright Office, September 1999, <http://www.loc.gov/copyright/circs/circ1.html#wci> (April 12, 2000).

13. The Digital Millennium Copyright Act, Overview, The UCLA Online Institute for Cyberspace Law and Policy, October 5, 1999, <http://www.gseis.ucla.edu/iclp/dmca1.htm> (August 26, 2000).

Chapter 8. Music Pirates

1. Mark Brown, "Record Companies Are Right (For Once): Napster Is Bad," *Rocky Mountain News*, May 7, 2000, p. 18D.

2. "Disabling the System," *Time Digital Page*, n.d., <http://www.time.com/time/digital/reports/mp3/frankel1.html> (June 25, 2000).

3. Chris Oakes, "MP3.com Fights Fire with Fire," *Wired Digital*, January 27, 2000, <http://www.wired.com/news/technology/0,1282,33952,00.html> (April 21, 2000).

4. Brown.

5. "War Against MP3 Player is Officially Over," *Time Digital Page*, August 5, 1999, <http://www.time.com/time/digital/daily/0,2822,29113,00.html> (August 26, 2000).

6. John Markoff, "Sony to Propose a Method for Protecting Digital Music," *The New York Times*, February 25, 1999, <http://www.nytimes.com/library/tech/99/02/biztech/articles/25sony.html> (April 21, 2000).

7. Ankarino Lara, "An Exclusive Interview with Ice-T," *ZDNet Music Page*, n.d., <http://music.zdnet.com/features/icet/> (June 23, 2000).

8. Oakes.

9. Mark Ward, "Why MP3 Piracy Is Much Bigger Than Napster," *BBC News Page*, February 13, 2001, <http://news.bbc.co.uk/hi/english/sci/tech/newsid_1168000/1168087.stm> (February 13, 2001).

10. Ned Potter, "If You Can't Beat 'Em...: Music Industry Joins Downloading Craze to Survive," *ABCNews.com Page*, March 9, 2000, <http://www.abcnews.go.com/onair/CloserLook/wnt_000309_CL_onlinemusic_feature.html> (April 21, 2000).

11. Frances Katz, Staff, "Web Deals to Expand Music Options," *The Atlanta Journal and Constitution*, June 12, 1999, p. A1.

12. Potter.

13. "Norwegian Teen Becomes Industry's Latest Test Case," Press Release, Electronic Frontier Foundation, January 25, 2000, <http://www.eff.org/IP/Video/DeCSS_prosecutions/ Johansen_DeCSS_case/20000125_eff_johansen_case_pressrel. html> (July 27, 2001).

14. Ian Harvey, "Netizens Rally Behind Teen Hacker," *The Toronto Sun*, January 8, 2000, p. 70.

15. Mike Snider, "DVD Piracy Ruling Could Alter Future of Digital Copyrights," *USA Today*, August 14, 2000, p. 3D.

16. "Don't Eat Pete," November 21, 2000, <http:// www.joeysmith.com/~jwecker> (February 10, 2001).

17. Lisa M. Bowman, "Nothing Says Free Speech Like Posting DVD-Hacking Code," *ZDNet News*, January 26, 2001, <http://www.zdnet.com/zdnn/stories/news/0,4586, 2679166,00.html> (February 10, 2001).

18. Lisa M. Bowman, "Web War Rages Over DVD-Cracking Site," *ZDNet News*, January 24, 2001, <http:// www.zdnet.com/zdnn/stories/news/0,4586,2678087,00. htm> (February 10, 2001).

19. Farhad Manjoo, "Court to Address DeCSS T-Shirt," *Wired Digital*, August 2, 2000, <http://www.wired.com/ news/technology/0,1282,37941,00.html> (August 25, 2000).

Chapter 9. Hackers

1. "You Can Get in Real Trouble for Hacking," *Kids Page*, U.S. Department of Justice, February 4, 1999, <http://www.usdoj.gov/kidspage/do-dont/reckless.htm> (July 1, 2000).

2. "Juvenile Computer Hacker Cuts Off FAA Tower," Press Release, U.S. Department of Justice, March 18, 1998, <http://www.usdoj.gov/criminal/cybercrime/ juvenilepld.htm> (July 1, 2000).

3. Linus Walleij, "Underground Hackers," *Copyright Does Not Exist*, October 30, 1999, <http://home.c2i.net /nirgendwo/cdne/ch4web.htm> (June 2, 2000).

4. Ibid.

5. Jeff Humphrey and Bruce C. Gabrielson, "Phreakers, Trashers and Hackers," Presentation at Air Force SEA Information Security Engineering Course, Burke, Virginia, June 1995, <http://www.blackmagic.com/ses/bruceg/ hackers.html> (June 2, 2000).

6. Walleij.

7. Dan Rather and Thalia Assuras, "Fifteen-Year-Old Canadian Arrested in Cyber Attack," CBS Evening News with Dan Rather, April 18, 2000.

8. "Two Charged in Britain with Stealing Credit Data Off of Web," *Minneapolis Star Tribune*, March 25, 2000, p. 6A.

9. Mike Meyers, "Cupid Costing Business Billions," *Minneapolis Star Tribune*, May 6, 2000, p. 1D.

10. Francine Kiefer, "Making the Punishment Fit the (Cyber)crime," *The Christian Science Monitor*, February 17, 2000, p. 4.

11. Louis J. Freeh, Congressional Testimony on Cybercrime, Senate Committee on Judiciary, Subcommittee for the Technology, Terrorism, and Government Information, Washington, D.C., March 28, 2000, <http://www.usdoj.gov/criminal/cybercrime/freeh328.htm> (April 14, 2000).

12. Humphrey and Gabrielson.

13. Doug Bedell, "Prying Into A Hacker's Mind: Many See Themselves as Good Guys Who Scorn Malicious Intruders," *The Dallas Morning News*, May 4, 2000, p. 1F.

14. Paul O'Donnell and Devin Gordon, "The FBI's War on Hackers," *Newsweek*, January 10, 2000, p. 8.

15. Chris Taylor, "Technology: Geeks Vs. G-Men—A Virtual Shooting War Breaks Out Between Hackers and the FBI. Are the Kids Really Worth the Trouble?" *Time*, June 14, 1999, p. 64.

16. Ibid.

17. Robert Scott, "Inside the World of 'Mafiaboy,'" *Maclean's*, May 1, 2000, p. 37.

18. Harry Bruinius, "It's Harder to Identify the Bad Guys Online," *The Christian Science Monitor*, March 28, 2000, <http://www.csmonitor.com/durable/2000/03/28/fp3s1csm.shtml> (March 29, 2000).

19. LOpht Heavy Industries, "Government Computer Security," Congressional Testimony, May 19, 1998.

20. Leslie Gevirtz, "Teen Computer Hackers Toss Electronic Spit Balls," *Reuters*, April 1, 1998.

Chapter 10. The Dark Side of the Internet

1. Tim Blangger, "Profitable Porn Spam Plagues E-Mail Users," *Newsday*, September 2, 1998, p. C2.

2. Howard Berkowitz, "Hate On The Internet," Statement Of The Anti-Defamation League on Hate on the Internet Before The Senate Committee on the Judiciary, Congressional Testimony, September 14, 1999.

3. "Ruling Against Anti-Abortion Website Raises Storm in US Over Rights," *The Irish Times*, February 4, 1999, <http://courses.cs.vt.edu/~cs3604/lib/Freedom.of.Speech/ Nuremburg.Irish.Times.html> (April 24, 2000).

4. Louis J. Freeh, Congressional Statement on Cybercrime, FBI Press Room, February 16, 2000, <http:// www.fbi.gov/pressrm/congress/congress00/cyber021600. htm> (July 1, 2000).

5. Tim Bryant, "Man Who Lured Girl On Internet Is Sent To Prison," *St. Louis Post-Dispatch*, July 25, 1998, p. 9.

6. David Finkelhor, Kimberly J. Mitchell, and Janis Wolak, *Online Victimization* (Alexandria, Virginia: National Center for Missing & Exploited Children, 2000), p. 35, <http://www.missingkids.com/html/onlinevictim_ report.html> (July 1, 2000).

7. Ibid., p. ix.

8. Ibid., pp. 2–4.

9. Debra Lynn Vial, "Gay Teenagers Easy Prey For Chat-Room Stalkers," *The Record* (Bergen County, N.J.), December 14, 1998, p. A1.

10. Telephone interview with Julie Posey, July 2, 2000.

11. J.M. Hirsch, "Cybersleuth Cop Attracts Pedophiles To His Web," *AP Online*, August 16, 1998, n.p.

12. Finkelhor, Mitchell, and Wolak, p. 8.

13. Ibid., p. 34.

Chapter 11. Looking Ahead

1. Tim Berners-Lee, *Weaving the Web* (San Francisco: HarperSanFrancisco, 1999), p. 4.

2. Ibid., p. 125.

Glossary

Clipper chip—A silicone chip that, when installed in a computer or digital device, would allow the government to decode any encryption used on that device.

cookie—A small text file which a Web site plants on a Web surfer's computer in order to collect information on that surfer.

copyright—Legal entitlement for creators to decide how their works will be used and to profit from what they have created.

cracker—Malicious hacker who breaks into systems and/or damages computer networks (see hacker).

cryptography—Keeping files and messages secure by mathematically turning text into a secret code.

cyphertext—Plain text which has been encoded into unreadable gibberish.

encryption—Turning text into code.

FTP—File Transfer Protocol, a tool for transferring files from one computer to another via the Internet.

hyperlink—Highlighted words or pictures on a Web page which link World Wide Web users to relevant information.

interoperable—Able to link computers and operating systems of all kinds.

IRC Chat—Internet Relay Chat, real-time conferencing on the Internet, also called a chat room.

ISP—Internet Service Provider, a computer's connection to the Internet.

newbie—Someone who is new to the Internet, a newsgroup, or hacking.

nexus—A business' physical point of presence—for example, a store or business office.

operating system—The software that runs the computer—for example, Windows and Linux.

pedophile—A person who preys on children as sexual objects.

phreaker—A person who learns everything he or she can about the telephone system, often with the goal of breaking into the system to make free telephone calls.

piracy—Copying copyrighted software program and selling or distributing copies for free.

profile—Collected information used to predict surfers' interests and to target them with appropriate online advertisements.

root access—Complete control of a network or system, usually only available to a system operator who knows the correct password.

shareware—Software that users can try out before they buy.

virus—A secretly planted program that can mess up the victim's computer.

war dialer—A cracking program that calls a large number of phone numbers and records those which answer with computer connect tones.

warez—Software that has been stripped of its copy protection and shared or sold.

Further Reading

Alpern, Andrew. *101 Questions About Copyright Law*. Mineola, N.Y.: Dover Publications, 1999.

Garfinkel, Simson, and Alan Schwartz, *Stopping Spam*. Cambridge, Mass.: O'Reilly & Associates, 1998.

Hill, Kevin A., and John E. Hughes. *Cyberpolitics: Citizen Activism in the Age of the Internet*. Lanham, Md.: Rowman & Littlefield Publishers, Inc., 1998.

Hull, Geoffrey P. *Recording Industry*. Upper Saddle River, N.J.: Prentice Hall, 1997.

Jennings, Charles and Debby Russell. *The Hundredth Window: Protecting Your Privacy and Security in the Age of the Internet*. New York: Free Press, 2000.

Naughton, John. *Brief History of the Future: From Radio Days to Internet Years in a Lifetime*. New York: Overlook Press, 2000.

Peck, Robert B. *Libraries, the First Amendment, and Cyberspace: What You Need To Know*. Chicago: American Library Association, 1999.

Young, Kimberly S. *Caught In The Net*. New York: John Wiley & Sons, 1998.

Internet Addresses

Anonymity
Anonymity and Privacy on the Internet
<http://www.stack.nl/~galactus>

Cheating and Plagiarism
Academic Misconduct & The Internet
<http://gsulaw.gsu.edu/lawand/papers/su98/
  misconduct>

The Instructors Guide To Internet Plagiarism
<http://www.plagiarized.com/index.shtml>

Internet Addiction
Center for Online Addiction, Help and Resources
<http://www.netaddiction.com>

Online Predators
Katie.com
> *The story of the first victim to successfully
> prosecute an Internet pedophile.*
<http://www.katiet.com>

Copyright on the Internet
Digital Millenium Copyright Act
<http://www.more.net/events/99consortium/
  presentation/dmca>

Domain Names and Cybersquatters
The Domain Name Rights Coalition
<http://www.netpolicy.com/dmainindex.html>

Index